**Meeting Special Educational
A Scottish Perspectiv**

Series Editors
Gwynedd Lloyd *and* Judith Watson

Volume Two

**Chosen with Care? - Responses to
Disturbing and Disruptive Behaviour**

Edited by Gwynedd Lloyd

Moray House Publications
Holyrood Road, Edinburgh
EH8 8AQ

Current and forthcoming titles in this series

Innovatory Practice and Severe Learning Difficulties
Edited by Judith Watson
Published 1991

Special Needs at 16+
Edited by Alison Closs
Due: Autumn 1992

Curriculum for All: 5-14 and Special Needs
Edited by Elizabeth Jordan
Due: Spring 1993

All rights reserved. No part of this publication may be reproduced, stored in a retrieval system, or transmitted in any form or by any means, electronic, mechanical, photocopying, recording or otherwise, without prior permission of Moray House Publications.

First published 1992
ISBN 0 9015 80 47 3
© Gwynedd Lloyd

Printed and bound by Bell and Bain Ltd, Glasgow

Contents

INTRODUCTION and Note on Gender
Gwynedd Lloyd — *v*

CHAPTER

1. Assessment - What is the Problem?
   Hamish McPhee — *1*

2. A Staff Development Approach to Improving Behaviour in Schools
   Alan McLean — *16*

3. Guidance
   Sandy Peterson — *33*

4. Developing a School Support Service for Children with Social, Emotional & Behavioural Difficulties
   Alan McLean and Joe Brown — *42*

5. Youth Strategies in Scotland
   Tim Pickles — *63*

6. Children's Hearings and School Problems
   Malcolm Schaffer — *74*

7. Panmure House School Groups: One Approach to Dealing with Young People's Schooling Difficulties
   Dave Simpson — *87*

8. Neighbourhood Projects and the School
   Barry Wilford — *98*

9. Residential Schools after List 'D'
   Andrew McCracken — *110*

10. Moving Towards Change. The Role of People, Place and Programme in Creating a Residential Therapeutic Environment for Children
    David Dean — *118*

11. Education in a Psychiatric Setting
    Deirdre Leach   *129*

12. Secure Provision
    Bill Duffy   *134*

Postscript: a story
   'Sur'
    Dougie McKenzie   *141*

CONTRIBUTORS   *148*

Introduction and Note on Gender
Gwynedd Lloyd

The title of this volume derives from the Report produced by HM Inspectors of Schools in Scotland, 'Choosing with Care' (1990). This report discussed, in fairly critical terms, '. . . provision for pupils with behavioural, emotional and social difficulties'. The survey conducted by the Inspectors found considerable variation in the pattern and type of provision, so that 'Pupils of comparable age and background, evincing similar problems, could be treated quite differently, depending upon where they happened to live.' They may also be dealt with differently according to the views or theoretical model held by professionals in the various systems in which they are involved.

This book looks at some of the provision available for children and young people whose behaviour is seen as disturbing and or disruptive. It does not attempt to set out any one view of the 'causes' of deviant behaviour, recognising that most accounts depend on the subjective perceptions or the theoretical position of the observer. It does reflect, however, a widespread willingness to recognise the sociological perspective on the issue, rather than relying on a purely psychologically based 'deficit' model of troubled or troublesome behaviour. Most, although perhaps not all, of the contributors would agree with the observations of MacPhee (Chapter 1). 'The area of "bad" behaviour is fraught with semantic problems. The terms used in the title of this volume may all be seen as problematic: disruptive; disturbing; special educational needs. The field is a mass of traps and paradoxes . . . .'

In every region of Scotland there is now a commitment to maintain children and young people in their own homes and neighbourhood schools and to see specialist provision as essentially short-term and focussed on the reintegration of pupils into their original school. A number of the chapters refer to the development of regional, collaborative youth strategies intended to promote this. There is still, however, an acknowledgement that there may still continue to be a small number of boys and girls whose needs cannot be met in mainstream education. For them we need to provide alternatives with a high quality of curriculum and care. Dean argues (Chapter 9) that '. . . there will always be a small proportion of any nation's children for whom the only responsible action is to immerse them in a radical alternative to their current lifestyle, which is at the root of their dysfunctioning and their distress.'

The authors of this book work across the spectrum of provision, from mainstream secondary schools to specialised residential settings. They have

Meeting Special Educational Needs:
A Scottish Perspective

different professional backgrounds in teaching, psychology, the law or social work. They share a considerable concern for the needs and rights of children and their families. I recognise that this is very much a book by professionals for professionals and wish, in retrospect, that perhaps the voices of young people and their families themselves could have been more apparent. It is also, in many chapters, written by service managers - by headteachers, project leaders, principal psychologists: a future book might consider the possibly different perspectives offered by class teachers, care and project workers.

The book does offer a picture of the developing provision in Scotland and an account of practice in very different kinds of setting. This kind of picture is not easily accessible to many professionals working in the field, many of whom will have a very partial knowledge of other approaches and resources. Consequently, decisions about the future of children and young people may be made sometimes in a relatively uninformed way, influenced by a particular professional bias or a habitual use of a familiar resource or strategy.

This book, like the others in this series, is concerned exclusively with the Scottish system. This is intended partly to rectify the tendency of books written about Britain to refer largely or exclusively to England and Wales, but also in recognition of the distinctive character of Scottish culture and the systems described here. While developments in Scotland in many ways parallel those in the rest of Britain, for example in the move away from more specialist and residential schools towards more community based responses, nevertheless there are identifiable differences. Education and social work are more homogeneous and centralised in Scotland, the national systems are smaller and more accessible and, while it is clearly possible to identify regional variation, still it may be argued that there is more standardisation of practice. Work with children and young people is deeply influenced by the welfare based Children's Hearing System. Pickles (Chapter 5), when discussing the development of regional youth strategies argues that they can be seen as 'uniquely Scottish'. 'Elsewhere in Britain, such collaborative practices tend to be restricted to particular aspects of work with children in difficulty such as child abuse or juvenile justice. The broader approach, which has always been an aspect of Scottish child care, has permitted the development of youth strategies . . . .'

There is no real evidence to suggest that the incidence of difficult behaviour, '. . . one of the most problematic areas to gauge statistically' (MacPhee Chapter 1) is any greater in Scottish schools although Johnstone and Munn (1992) found that according to teachers 'The same kinds of pupil behaviours occurred in both sets of schools and classrooms, in about the same frequency overall, but apparently on a higher daily basis in Scottish schools.' Scottish teachers also expressed '. . . a more pessimistic view than Scottish headteachers.' Scottish teachers were also more worried about cheeky remarks. 'This could imply that the English/Welsh child is more polite or subdued than his Scottish cousin, or it could imply that Scottish teachers are more liable to pick up such behaviour . . .' or '. . . that the Scottish teacher has a stricter definition of what constitutes cheek' (Johnstone and Munn op cit).

In Chapter 1 Hamish MacPhee argues that '. . . evidence might lead to the conclusion that incidence is not simply child-centred but depends on the context of the school, the mechanisms for assessment, resources for placement and for dealing with difficult behaviour as well as curricular, family and peer group factors.' He discusses the problems and issues involved in assessment, arguing that the '. . . framing of the questions has the greatest bearing on assessment outcome.' He is critical of a needs based model, pointing out that SEN legislation and the '. . . nature of the Recording or statementing procedure located the problem in or around the child.' Often this obscures '. . . systemic, policy or resource issues.' He argues for the adoption of a model '. . . setting out rights as principles of practice and assessment.'

Alan McLean in Chapter 2 refers to teachers' concerns about dealing with disruptive behaviour in schools and describes the development of two packages of in-service materials designed to help teachers '. . . to be more effective classroom managers.' The approach is based on '. . . identified effective practice and school processes related to good pupil behaviour.' The programmes are school and teacher based and emphasise the prevention of disruptive behaviour. The three key assumptions are

'1. Class teachers have the central responsibility for their own classroom discipline.
2. Teacher behaviour has a large influence on their pupils' behaviour.
3. Positive group management skills can be described, practised and acquired.'

The approach brings together findings from academic research with '. . . the most important resource- the collective experience and expertise of participants.'

Sandy Peterson in Chapter 3 develops a critical view of the Scottish secondary school guidance system from the perspective of a committed practitioner. He outlines the arguments and confusions over the role of guidance, in particular those between care and control, support and discipline. He goes on to consider some of the main approaches used by guidance teachers ie counselling, behaviour contracts, groupwork and social education, and to argue for consistency, for '. . . clarity and honesty in guidance work.'

Introduction

In Chapter 4 Alan McLean and Joe Brown describe the '... rationale for and the development of teaching support services for children with social, emotional and behavioural difficulties within mainstream schools in Strathclyde region.' They develop a critique of segregated provision and support the view of the Inspectors expressed in 'Choosing with Care'(1990) that '... the aim must be to prevent the need for alternative education rather than anticipate it.' They discuss the problems and issues created by the existence of a separate service and emphasise that 'Providing a specialist sector support must not reinforce the common notion that behaviour is distinct from learning, detached from the curriculum and beyond the teacher's influence and responsibility. They argue that behaviour support should be seen as part of general support services and in particular as linked with learning support. The emphasis is on "learning skills" rather than on "behaviour change".'

Tim Pickles in Chapter 5 gives an account of the development of collaborative youth strategies, identifying the Children's Hearing System, the Intermediate Treatment Resource Centre (regrettably now closed), and the move away from the use of the nationally funded List D schools, as the background to regional initiatives promoting the use and development of community resources and the development of inter-professional working. He identifies the practical problems of cooperative work between professionals with different training and different agency priorities but emphasises the value and success of the strategies.

In Chapter 6 Malcolm Schaffer discusses the role of the Children's Hearing System in dealing with school related issues, not just that of non-attendance which is a ground of referral to a hearing, but also in recognition that education is an important aspect of the lives of all the children and young people referred. He argues that 'Research has demonstrated that the school's input is a crucial aspect of the Children's Hearing's decision making (Martin ,Fox & Murray 1981). In 91% of the cases studied, schooling featured as a main topic of discussion....' He concludes that '... the education profession is a core ingredient of the Children's Hearing System , with an essential role in helping the identification of what is in the best interests of the child.'

Dave Simpson in Chapter 7 continues the theme of collaborative interprofessional practice and youth strategies with an account of the Panmure House school groups. He argues that 'The Youth Strategy initiatives have stimulated the development of imaginative and creative in-school strategies geared towards meeting the needs of all young people.' There remain, however a minority of young people who '... require a different and more intensive type of experience than schools could offer.' The school groups attempt to balance the need to maintain contact with mainstream schools, while offering an alternative programme with an emphasis on groupwork and family work.

In Chapter 8 Barry Wilford offers practical examples of the way in which a neighbourhood youth social work project can work with young people in difficulty at school. He offers models of intervention including individual support of young people, groupwork, and the application of a broad based youth work approach to work in the classroom. He identifies the strengths of projects in the voluntary sector and argues that there is increasing recognition of the value of youth work methods and curricula within, as well as complementary to, school curricula.

Andrew McCracken in Chapter 9 discusses the new role of the former List 'D' residential schools '... within the context of developing strategies based on the community.' He describes the '... present mixed economy in terms of ownership, management and registration ... mirrored by considerable variation in both types and numbers of schools.' He sees the future in terms of the development of flexible and imaginative '... programmes of care and education which are matched to the individual's needs and circumstances.' Schools will have their place in a range of residential services used by regions, '... from schools which offer secure conditions ... to the therapeutic schools .... The former List "D" schools occupy a broad middle ground along with, and no longer distinguishable from, a number of the List "G" schools.'

In Chapter 10 we reproduce a paper first given by David Dean in Moscow. Raddery represents the therapeutic end of the spectrum of residential schools. Dean uses the categories of People, Place and Programme to look at '... the work of a school/community for emotionally damaged children.' Unlike much of the provision described in this book, Raddery operates within one clear theoretical perspective, offering a psychotherapeutic approach to work with children, described as 'psychologically disfunctioning', 'maladjusted' and 'emotionally damaged'. Dean argues for a holistic approach with concern for every detail of the programme and environment of the community.

Deirdre Leach in Chapter 11 examines a residential psychiatric setting, offering a small number of children '... a badly needed period of respite and time for family therapy in the hope of restoring the family intact.' She argues for a balanced view of child psychiatry, through a resolution of the traditional differences and debates between professionals, within and outside the hospital setting and makes a plea for more research into the place of education in psychiatric units.

In Chapter 12 Bill Duffy looks at the background to the development of secure provision and the reasons for admission. He argues that since the opening of the first secure unit at Rossie in 1962 '... we have shown an increasing tendency as a society to lock up young people', secure provision now forming a larger proportion of residential school places. He then describes how St Mary's addresses a major issue common to much of the provision described in this book, i.e. how to '... provide a balanced curriculum, which would aim to offer a range of educational experiences, common to all pupils of the same age and ability, as well as catering for the specific individual circumstances of each pupil.'

Introduction

This last point typifies the issue faced by all the contributors to this book - how to offer high quality and special experiences to children and young people in difficulty without separating them unecessarily from their peers, and how to maintain as far as possible their access to mainstream curricula. The book as a whole reflects a greater expectation that ordinary schools and teachers will be willing to take more responsibility for pupils with 'emotional or behavioural difficulties', through exploring effective classroom management strategies and institutional responses. It represents a commitment to maintaining children and young people in their own homes and communities where possible, but also to the provision of high quality, varied and flexible alternatives for the small numbers who may need special care and education.

Note on Gender.

'... A woman's sexuality is central to the way she is judged.' (Lees 1989)

'Most provision was nominally available equally to both boys and girls but in practice boys equalled girls in a ratio of about 4:1.' (HMI 1990)

Of the great number of books published in the last twenty or so years on the question of deviance in school very few have explicitly considered girls. More has been written in the field of youth culture and on the question of juvenile justice but nevertheless it is still the case that girls continue to be relatively invisible. Many books referring to 'children', 'young people' or 'kids' turn out in fact to be about boys. The intention of this note is to put, at the front rather than the back of the reader's mind, the question of whether girls' deviance is different from boys', and to assert that there are important issues that need to be considered about how we understand and respond to girls within the kind of provision described in this book.

One widely held view is that women and girls who are deviant must be especially deviant, offending against not only general standards of acceptable behaviour but also against accepted notions of femininity. 'Since women and girls generally do not commit crimes, those who do must be very bad or sick.' (Gelsthorpe 1986) Many of the teachers and other professionals interviewed as part of my own research expressed views along the lines of '... a bad girl is worse than a bad boy.'

Girls are less likely than boys to be referred for sanctions, or to be excluded from school, for overtly disruptive behaviour. In our survey of school liaison groups in Lothian Region (Lloyd & Cohen 1990), we found that boys were three times as likely to have been excluded. While a smaller number of girls were referred to the School Liaison Groups, they were, however, referred for a similar pattern of reasons, with disruptiveness the most frequent. It seems though that girls are less likely to express disaffection with school in aggressively disruptive behaviour but more in a subversive manipulation of time and space. In a series of interviews with girls focussing on how girls get into 'bother' at school the girls '... enjoyed telling of their more dramatic confrontations with teachers, putting a cake into a teacher's face, hitting teachers and fighting in class.' However, although '... about half of the girls in this study were seen by their school as extremely disruptive it became clear that the girls saw "bother" mainly as a result of persistent everyday misbehaviour - talking, smoking, not wearing "suitable" clothes, lateness and some absence and generally resisting the attempts of the school to contain them.' (Lloyd 1992)

The girls saw physical fighting as an acceptable, normal way of resolving disputes or defending their reputation but were less likely to introduce this into the classroom. They described some girls who had been in trouble in school for fighting as like 'laddies'. '... Lynn, she's always getting into trouble in class - she's too much like a laddie, fighting in class and that...' (Lloyd 1992) This view of some deviant girls as unfeminine corresponds to the view often expressed by professionals about girls who commit offences. Accounts from the 1960s of girl delinquents often suggested a common unfeminine physical type or appearance, for example Cowie et al (1968) generalise about delinquent girls as unattractive and overweight. These accounts also often see girls as less rational in their actions than boys or men and their behaviour as more emotionally or hormonally derived. These views were associated with methods, employed for example in the Scottish List 'D' schools for girls, which emphasised the development of feminine characteristics and personal appearance along with household skills, the latter involving considerable responsibility for the cleanliness of the schools.

While this view has been modified over the intervening years, it is still the case that referral of adolescent girls to specialised provision is much more likely to involve concern about their sexuality and their sexual behaviour, than is the case for the equivalent boys. This concern may be associated with a subjective view on the part of professionals about the nature of 'promiscuity' and its origins in an uncontrolled female sexuality. Adolescent girls have often been described as being in a double bind of the dual pressure to be sexually attractive but not too available. 'The girls tread a very narrow line. They must not end up being called a slag. But equally they do not want to be thought unapproachable, sexually cold - a "tight bitch"' (Lees 1989). Sexual behaviour is not often a focus of professional concern in boys. 'As long as boys' sexual behaviour is heterosexual their sexuality remains unproblematic; it is "natural" and thus does not merit attention' (Hudson 1989). The double bind for professionals here is to protect the interests of girls vulnerable to sexual exploitation while avoiding judgmental decisions about their behaviour.

If we look at referrals to the Children's Hearing System it is clear that whereas over five times as many boys as girls are referred to the Reporter for offences, boys and girls are referred in roughly similar numbers on non-offence grounds (SED 1991). In 1989 boys were referred on offence grounds at a rate of 43.6 per 1,000 (of 8-15 year olds) and on non-offence grounds at a rate of 11 per 1,000, girls on offence grounds at 7.9 per 1,000 (of 8-15 year olds) and non-offence grounds at 10.2 per 1,000. So there are more referrals of girls on non-offence grounds than on offence grounds. (For an explanation of the grounds for referral see Chapter 6 of this book.) Unfortunately the SED Statistical Bulletin does not differentiate between the different non-offence grounds which include non-attendance at school as well as beyond control and care and protection. A further helpful analysis by the SED of Table 15C in the 1991 Statistical Bulletin (Children under a supervision requirement at June 1989 by sex and type of referral for selected grounds of original referral) does suggest that once a decision has been made for a supervision order on grounds of beyond control or care and protection, then the kind of disposal will be similar for boys and girls.

There are a number of questions that could be investigated through future statistics. Are girls more likely to be referred on to a Hearing by Reporters and are they more likely to be subject to supervision orders? More difficult to establish but no less worth investigating is the importance of information about girls' sexual behaviour in influencing decisions when they have been referred on other grounds. It seems from my current research on girls in specialised provision, that they may often be referred on grounds of offence or of non-attendance but that the significant background to the decision is the professionals' concern about their sexual behaviour or their fears or suspicions of sexual abuse unsupported by adequate evidence to proceed on those grounds.

A quick analysis by one principal of a girls', former List 'D', school of the reasons for referral of his current population was as follows.

> Beyond parental control - 3 girls.
> Beyond parental control + non-attendance- 2.
> Non-attendance -2
> Non-attendance + care and protection -1
> Non-attendance +disruptiveness at school -1
> Non-attendance +disruptiveness in children's home -1
> Disruptive in children's home- 1
> Non-attendance +drug misuse -1
> Non-attendance + theft- 2
> Theft- 1

Care and protection -1
Promiscuity+?sexual abuse- 1
Incest -1.

Petrie (1986) in her study of girls in a Scottish List 'D' school states that the most common reason for referral was absence from school. She argues that while both boys and girls may cause concern over absence from school 'Absentee boys tend to get into mischief... but absentee girls seem to attract anxiety over their sexual safety.' She does find some evidence of incest and suggests a need for further research in this area.

There is sometimes in schools, especially perhaps in co-educational residential schools, a confusion among staff as to whether they are dealing with victims or the guilty. On a recent visit to such a school a senior member of staff remarked smiling, 'Of course, they're all whores' and a teacher in the same school disclosed, in the hearing of his class 'The girls have all been sexually abused.' I have no idea about the substance of either of these remarks but they do indicate a general view that girls in specialised provision are all there for one or both of these reasons. It is easy for this to slip into a suggestion that if they were sexually abused perhaps in some way their own sexuality was at least partly to blame. 'The myth that children are seductive is the commonest device by which a society can rationalise the occurrence of child sexual abuse, and operates in much the same way as the notion that adults who get harrassed must have "asked for it"' (Driver 1989).

In many accounts of 'problem' girls there is still an emphasis on what Hudson (1989) calls the 'psychopathological paradigms'. Recent provision for young people with 'emotional or behavioural difficulties' has, as I argued in the Introduction, reflected a shift to an awareness of sociologically based accounts of deviant behaviour, focussing on disadvantage, on class, culture and institutional effectiveness. These factors seem to be less often considered, however, in the discussion of girls. When professionals express the view, mentioned earlier, that girls are more difficult to work with, it is often because of '...their apparent mood-swings, non-rationality, outbursts of aggression, and internalisation of emotional discontents...'(Hudson 1989). Such behaviour is understood to reflect an emotional imbalance rather than an understandable way of dealing with their lives. Hudson argues that '... emotionality as a means of social communication and expression should be seen not as a sign of deficient personality but rather as a positive response.' Petrie in her study of girls in Scottish List 'D' schools, argues that we need further research using a 'psycho-social model'.

In attempting to bring the issue of gender to the forefront of this book I wanted to argue that there are important questions for professionals to consider. We need to look at our explanations of deviant behaviour in terms of the social

Introduction

construction of gender roles. We need to ask whether in our decision making we are applying different criteria to boys and girls and if so whether we do so consciously and in the best interests of girls. We need to look at co-educational provision in terms of whether it meets and reflects the needs of girls. We need to look at the curriculum of special schools and units in terms of whether it reflects the concerns of girls. We should consider whether girls are appropriately placed in schools where they are only a very small proportion of the overall population (see Houston 1987). We need to look at the increasing use of secure accommodation for girls - in the year to March 1991 60 girls and 142 boys were admitted, a much bigger proportion of girls than in other forms of residential care.

It is important to recognise that there are also issues here to do with boys - there are important questions about boys' deviance that are to do with our definitions of masculinity. We need to acknowledge the issue of gender as central, not marginal, to our understanding of troubled and troublesome behaviour in boys and girls.

References

Booth,T, Swann,S, Masterton,M and Potts,P(eds) (1992). *Curricula for Diversity in Education.* Routledge.

Cain,M(ed) (1989). *Growing Up Good.* Sage

Cowie.J, Cowie,V and Slater,E (1968). *Delinquency in Girls.* Heinemann.

Driver,E (1989). *Child Sexual Abuse, Feminist Perspectives.* Macmillan

Gelsthorpe, L (1989). *Sexism and the Female Offender.* Gower.

Houston,J (1987). *Placing Girls in List 'G' Schools.* SED/RPI.

Hudson, A (1989). Troublesome girls. In Cain (ed).

Johnstone, M and Munn,P (1992). *Discipline in Scottish Secondary Schools.* SCRE.

Lees, S (1989). Learning to love. In Cain (ed).

Lloyd,G (1992). Lassies of Leith talk about bother. In Booth, et al (eds).

Petrie,C (1986). *The Nowhere Girls.* Gower.

S.E.D. (1991). Referrals of children to Reporters and Children's Hearings 1989. *Statistical Bulletin.*

Assessment - What is the Problem?

Hamish MacPhee

Assessment remains a 'hot' issue in the field of education, and among educational psychologists in particular. Despite the arguments set against traditional assessment over a long period of time (Maliphant 1982, Feiler 1988), for many teachers and workers dealing with difficult pupils the issues are not clear. This paper is an attempt to summarise some of these issues with regard to the assessment and identification of disturbing and difficult pupils.

It is fairly traditional to approach the issue of assessment with a description or definition. Examination of the literature reveals a large number of definitions all of which carry value laden assumptions. In the circumstances, it may be appropriate to propose a definition which expresses some of the author's value bias.

Assessment may be construed as a description of the process of helping young people in difficult situations. Such a description would include a statement of the resources used to help address the problems, and the identification of resources which might help further. Such a definition does not locate the problem in the child, the family or in the 'system', but in the process of change. This type of approach to assessment also challenges the notion that assessment and identification are stages which lead to 'treatment' and placement; the emphasis here is on resources and problem solving.

In the following sections, issues will be discussed in relation to the development of thinking on assessment and identification. It will be argued that assessment should be seen as a problem solving process which carries on through a period of intervention with a child and family in context. This is not a new formulation (Wilson 1984, McGuckin 1983, Tomlinson 1982), but there has been a tendency for statements about the need for contextual or ecological assessment to be followed by definitions or methods of assessment which appear in many ways to be child based e.g. Hoghughi (1980).

The description of assessment outlined in this paper departs strongly from the traditional child deficit models. Such a change in emphasis raises a number of issues including the role of resources, theoretical stance, inter-professional working, policy agreement, the role of parents and young people, the role of experts, the assumptions structure of the assessment process, etc.

Chapter 1

The who, what, why and where debate

Assessment and identification questions are often stated in terms of who, what, why and where (Draper 1987). This range of questions might include issues such as:

> who is to be assessed?
> who will take part in the assessment?
> who will use/have access to the assessment?
> what is the aim of the assessment?
> what is the likely outcome(s)?
> what is the framework of the assessment?
> what has been (can be) done to help?
> why is the assessment needed?
> where is the assessment to take place?

It can be argued that the framing of these questions in itself has the greatest bearing on assessment outcome (Frederickson 1991).

Each of the questions can be developed along particular lines or values. 'What is the aim?', can be addressed in a number of ways, e.g. labelling for 'treatment' or as 'in need'. The examination of how 'wh' questions are addressed can lead to an examination of the role of professionals, their interface, the control of resources, the framework or structure in which the assessment and identification occur, and the methods and language of assessment.

The language of assessment

The area of 'bad' behaviour is fraught with semantic problems. The terms used in the title of this volume may all be seen as problematic: disruptive; disturbing; special educational needs. The field is a mass of traps and paradoxes, e.g. to be assessed one has to have been identified as in need of assessment which implies prior assessment.

This might appear to imply that assessment is a complex process in which labels (if used) are applied after due consideration. In some instances, however, all that might be required to produce a label which implies future needs, placements and plans, is a single event e.g. exclusion from school. McManus (1980) has argued that in some schools and authorities, the label 'excluded' has a highly predictive value with regard to future education and placement. At the same time, there exists a large body of evidence to show that exclusion is heavily influenced by systematic factors (Reynolds 1981, Galloway 1985, McLean 1987, MacPhee 1987).

The language of assessment and its child centred focus are evident in traditional assessment and referral processes: 'Child X is to be referred for assessment'. This can result in a model of assessment where a problem (pupil?) is to be assessed by professionals using a variety of 'expert' methods to arrive at a prescription, recommendation for treatment, or placement. Examination of the language of assessment requires a discussion of a number of issues including: the relationship of theory to assessment methods; the contribution of professional status; and, the multi-disciplinary process. Changes in the language of assessment can imply changes in value system, the consideration of ethics in assessment, and in particular, the young person's rights.

If the process of identification and assessment were purely child centred and free from institutional, policy and resource constraints then one could expect similar levels of incidence of a particular label group or syndrome across regions and across schools. it is useful, therefore, to examine the evidence on incidence as a clue to the parameters defining the frequency of identification and 'need' for assessment.

Identification and incidence

In comparison to other areas of education it might be felt that the quantification of the incidence of difficult behaviour would be a relatively easy matter. Behaviour problems may be perceived as identifying themselves. The incidence of difficult behaviour is one of the most problematic areas to gauge statistically.

On a small scale Gillham (1978) has shown that teachers and parents both identify around 7% of the school population as difficult (or maladjusted), but that these are in effect *different* seven percents. Other surveys have shown large differences in reports of difficult behaviour, need for assessment, and need for placement (McManus 1980, Tattum 1978). Such difficulties, and variations indicate the interactive, systematic and subjective nature of many of the labels applied to behaviour. These problems have been referred to by Graham (1989) and Choosing with Care (H.M.S.O. 1990). Both documents refer to the problems in separating causes and effects of difficult behaviour.

Exclusion is a particularly important event in influencing placement in day and residential places. At the same time exclusion rates have been shown to vary greatly between schools in ways that cannot be accounted for in terms of catchment, deprivation, academic bias or other factors (Reynolds 1981, Galloway 1987, McLean 1987). In addition to within school factors, rates of exclusion are heavily influenced by regional rules and procedures, as are patterns of placement (MacPhee 1987).

Evidence regarding the subjective and socially defined nature of assessment and identification can also be found in studies of difficult behaviour which take gender into account. Not only are girls less likely to be assessed or identified as in need of placement, they are also likely to be treated differently if they are assessed (Houston 1987, McManus 1987). In many regions where there is no residential provision for girls, none are ever identified as being in need of such placements.

In essence, the evidence might lead to the conclusion that incidence is not simply child centred, but depends on the context of the school, the mechanisms for assessment, resources for placement and for dealing with difficult behaviour, as well as curricular, family and peer group factors. A number of studies have concluded that there is little evidence of an overall increase in difficult behaviour, rather there is an increase in special provision and placements designed to deal with such behaviour - perhaps out of context (Graham (1988), Topping (1983), Munn and Johnston (1987)). Several of these authors also imply that this awareness in turn feeds the need for further increases in assessment to fill the available places.

Assessment methods

A comprehensive review of the relationship between theories and methods of assessment is beyond the range of this paper (see Hoghughi's 1980 summary). It is important to remember, however, that professionals frequently carry out assessments within a theoretical framework. This means that those who adhere primarily to behaviourist, humanistic, psychodynamic, interactionist, social learning or other theories will deliver the assessment within this framework. This may pose problems for any joint decision making or joint assessment in that the languages of these approaches may be different, and the outcomes of such assessments may be less (or more) open to mutual debate.

For example, the label 'severe depression of adolescence', may have meaning and predictive power in one of these frameworks but not in another. It may also have meaning for one professional and not for others (it may have little meaning outside of the 'expert' circle).

The more theory laden and 'expert' the assessment method and subsequent outcome, the less likely that it will be open to joint negotiation and discussion, particularly by the young person, their family, or school staff. Such problems have raised questions about specialised assessment methods and have led to the popularisation of check lists, behaviour scales and other 'objective' measures which appear to have more face validity in that they appear to actually sample the observed behaviour (Gillham 1978).

More recently, however, questions have been raised regarding how objective 'objective' checklists and measures can be, at the most obvious level they are open to observer bias. For example, it has been shown that when observed by a neutral observer pupils identified by teachers as difficult were differentiated from their peers not by rate of misbehaviour, but by their likelihood of receiving a teacher reprimand (Frude & Gault, 1984).

There is also a danger that the strength of these checklists, and assessment tasks - (face validity) can make them appear to be 'true' or value free. In fact interpretation and expert views arising from such methods are as open to value system bias as any other method (Tizard 1990, Jeffries 1990). These methods also have the disadvantage of being context specific and static, ie. they may not reflect the changing nature of a particular problem. In addition they do, in the main tend to be child focussed, and therefore can strengthen the tendency to follow a child deficit model (Feiler 1988).

The structure of assessment

In the 1960's and 1970's the model of assessment of difficult youngsters moved on from the separate individual test or assessment towards multi-disciplinary assessment in an 'assessment centre'. In these centres young people identified as having a variety of social, behavioural and emotional problems would be assessed in a specialised residential setting by a team of professionals including education, social work, psychological service, and psychiatric staff.

This development appeared to be a significant step forward in terms of co-ordination of assessment plans, reports and recommendations. It had a strong appeal to many and was (and is) used by the Children's Hearing system as a way of obtaining "an assessment". The structure of this type of assessment has disadvantages too. McGuckin (1983) produced a paper which clearly expresses some of these concerns. In this paper he challenges the notion that assessment can be taken out of context and argues that if it is to be useful it has to have meaning in the young persons 'real' world. Central to McGuckin's argument is that assessment should not be seen as a separate 'bolt on' to the process of helping in troubled situations, but a part of that process. This dynamic, process view of assessment contrasts sharply with the static, expert package, view which had developed.

The assessment centre model was co-ordinated, and usually resulted in an agreed report or recommendation. The resulting document was invariably child focussed and aimed at treating or rectifying identified deficits. Such a perspective can ignore important contextual or systematic variables (Tutt 1978). This type of assessment also had little control over the context of many of the situations affecting the child, and more importantly lacked control of possible resources and resourcing. Assessment frequently became assessment for placement. Wilson (1981) argued that this 'best fit' placement model, was frequently not in the best interests of the young person, but resulted in an attempt to match people to places. There had been (and still is) little evaluation of the effectiveness of the match or outcome in many cases. Where evaluation was carried out the results are not always reassuring (Fisher 1978, Tutt 1981). Wilson also promoted the idea that such assessments should be aimed at a full consideration of the child's needs. The idea that resources should be examined with regard to the child's needs was then the focus in legislation and professional practice in the late 70's and 80's.

The concept of Special Educational Needs was incorporated in legislation as a result of the Warnock Report (1978) and this systematised the assessment of 'need'. This formulation appeared to move assessment on, in that it formally linked the notion of examining the issue of resourcing with regard to the child's context; and away from a simple child deficit/best fit for placement models. The Special Needs legislation was still largely child focussed, and the nature of the Recording or Statementing procedure located the problem in and around the child. Critics have argued that Special Needs often attributed to the child and their families are often systemic, resource, or policy issues (Galloway and Goodwin 1978, Tomlinson 1982).

The notion of needs, in conjunction with concern about the process and context of assessment have helped develop the notion of community based assessment. Community assessment, as McGuckin has advocated, suggests that the presenting problem should be examined in its context. In ideal terms this means that the 'whole' problem can be assessed and that resources can be tailored to the situation.

Multi-disciplinary assessment and communication

The benefits of bringing professionals together to contribute to assessments have been a feature of most assessment systems whether they are test based, child centred, placement centred, or needs centred. It has also been much advocated in professional papers and in Government Reports (H.M.I. Choosing with Care, 1989, Warnock 1978). The assessment centre often acts or acted as a focus for this group and the assessment centre head often acted as a co-ordinator of this group.

Despite this, and the common sense appeal of its advantages, multi-disciplinary assessment is often seen as problematic and 'more advocated than practiced' (Pickles 1990). Why then, is the process so difficult? Once again the reasons lie in the language of the assessment, access to that language, the control of resources, agreement on policy regarding acceptable outcomes, agreement on the role of parents etc. Where agencies come together with different policies, and means of expressing these policies, then problems can develop. Equally where agencies do not share resourcing or may disagree about the need for evaluation of resourcing then the multi-disciplinary process may be doomed from the outset (Pickles and Gill 1990).

The bringing together of different professionals highlights the issues of agreed means of communication, agreed aims or means of judging outcomes, and mutual influence in the decision making process. This will clearly grind to a halt if differences in any of these areas are too great. If one professional feels that the issue is a child based pathology, while another feels it is a problem in the family, while another sees the main issue as a school system problem, the process will be difficult and agreement unlikely. There is a danger in these instances that the differences in policy; resourcing; or inter-professional issues; are ignored and it becomes easy to focus on a child deficit or 'needs' model (Galloway 1985).

Agreement in policy regarding resourcing and the management of difficult behaviour within an authority can ease this problem. The benefits to the process of assessment and of helping young people by agreeing a framework of policy and resourcing have been argued by Allen and Fearon (1989). With this in mind and several authorities in Scotland have produced policy documents on young people which are agreed by various agencies within the authority and provide a focus for joint action.

Much of the discussion has concerned professionals and their framework for action. In addition, it is necessary to consider the ethics of the decision making process and of assessment. Does the young person have rights? Does the young person have a genuine place in the assessment process? What part does the young person's family have to play? Galloway (1985) has pointed out that it may appear to be acceptable to refer to maladjusted pupils, but is it acceptable to talk of deviant schools, or as teachers or psychologists as maladjusted? Once more there may be social or inter-agency pressure which ensures that a child focussed deficit model is adopted.

Multi-professional working can be a double edged sword, it can lead to the challenging of insular beliefs and can help add differing perspectives to a problem. On the other hand it can serve to justify the role of 'experts' who make predictions about future behaviour on the basis of agreed labels (the accuracy of these predictions may not be evaluated). The Needs model may not help in this as it can focus the 'experts' efforts in the identification of areas where the child is not coping and therefore where his/her needs lie.

An alternative value system might be to assess what has been done to help improve the situation and to collectively examine which resources could be deployed to change the situation further. Multi-disciplinary assessment can only operate effectively if there is joint access to communication, decision making and resourcing. This also implies the effective evaluation of data regarding outcomes back into the system to influence future views. The process must also include the young person and his/her parents. 'Assessment can and should aim to build upon the resources and insights of the people being assessed, as well as the assessors' Wilson 1991). It is possible that the divisions between professionals, and between assessor and assessed, would be less relevant if the process was restated in terms of a description of attempts to help improve a difficult situation, and to develop hypotheses about that situation.

Chapter 1

Needs, rights and principles

The change in the focus or framework for assessment and identification can be seen as paralleling the development of thinking in various professions. This is especially true with regard to educational psychology where there has been a well documented trend from a child deficit, labelling, assess-treat-place, model towards a more contextual model (Gillham 1975, Jones and Freiderickson 1990). This has also been accompanied by a move away from testing towards approaches which are more naturalistic and ecological (Maliphant 1972, Freiderickson 1991). In these formalisations, assessment and evaluation have as much meaning in institutional and systematic terms as in terms of the individuals. Once again this has been influenced by doubts about the effectiveness of the 'treatment' model (Tutt, 1978, Galloway and Goodwin, 1978).

As we have seen, the framework for assessment moved from an ascertainment of handicap model towards a 'best fit' for placement model. In turn this was replaced by the concept of special educational needs. Some of the positive concepts of this approach were discussed earlier. This model explicitly took into account the views of the parents and the young person and allowed them access to (some of) the documentation. The focus was also changed from one of handicap to that of resources to be considered in assessment.

The special needs approach does raise ethical issues, the legislation did not provide a direct link between needs and the funding of resources. The assessment process implied by the needs model was explicitly child focussed and implied the collation of evidence about how the child faired in a number of domains, social, cognitive, academic etc. Galloway (1985) has argued that this could amount to a tailoring of the 'needs' document to fit the resources which would have been provided anyway, not 'new' resources. Other authors have agreed that the formal process of recording needs can act to deny some rights and freedoms which the young person might enjoy otherwise e.g. choice of school (Swanson 1984).

The 'needs' approach can also lead to the omission of contextual variables; for example in a high exclusion school, a very large number of pupils may be identified as 'in need' of assessment or alternative placement, whereas in a different school or with different supports in the school few pupils would 'need' such intervention. Tutt (1984) has also pointed out that when the S.E.D. proposes that up to 55% of the school population may have special needs, it is possible to question the system of delivery in ordinary schools. In many ways this parallels debates in the context of learning difficulties regarding the allocation of time to curriculum support and/or individual help.

The framework for analysis in assessment was developed by the needs model but left concerns about the individual focus of the process, and the comparative lack of contextual emphasis. For some, the needs model of assessment was a deficit model in humanitarian guise (Solity 1991). The problems with the needs model and its predecessors has led to discussion of the importance of rights in the context of work with, and assessment of, young people. This approach has been recently outlined by Kirkcaldy (1989), who suggests that notions of the pragmatics of placement, and need, should be considered in the light of the rights of the young person. The rights model has also found favour in national and international legislation (Trump 1991).

Kirkcaldy questions the validity of pragmatic evaluative notions in some aspects of decision making, and draws the parallel between this and the notion of the evaluation of a woman's right to vote. It is significant that this paper has been accepted as a position statement by the Scottish Division of Educational and Child Psychology. In practice, the rights model would set out the parameters under which assessment and decision making should be made. An example given might be 'each child's right to access to the education provision available to other children of the same age'. The advantage of the model is that it would contextualise the problem and build in resource implications. The rights model does not locate the problem in the child, the family, or in the system but sets the framework for problem solving and hypothesis testing. Conceptually it is also more powerful as it is more problematic to deny a right than to say that a need cannot be met (due to resource or other limitations).

At present, in many regions in Scotland the decision to record a child's needs or to complete an assessment with this in mind is taken after the destination is known; for example when a child is to be placed in a particular school a record is opened only after the place has been allocated and resources provided. The rights model would pose problems for this kind of pragmatic decision making. The rights model may also help promote integration whereas there is evidence that the needs model may have had the opposite effect (Tutt 1984, Galloway 1987, Solity 1991).

The emergence of the notion of rights was anticipated by Sayer in 1983: 'The individual statements of the 1981 act would not be needed if a school were committed to providing for all children, and the local authority were committed to resourcing the school so to do'. The rights model and the notion of rights, despite its recent development is not without its critics, and there are clear conceptual problems, some of these have been outlined by Trump (1991). If *processes* are not different then there is a chance that the relativism of the needs argument may also apply to the rights model.

There are dangers that rights are set out in such general terms that they are broadly agreeable to all, but do not translate into action. There is also the problem of what are, and what should be, rights. In the context of assessment it could be that the young person's rights are what they would have received anyway.

Resources, decision making and the assessment process must be shaped by articulated and agreed rights if change is to be effected. It may be that the emotive nature of 'rights' could make agreement on specific rights difficult to achieve if this implied changes in professional power or resourcing.

A way out of the possible impasse may be to set out the 'rights' as principles of practice and assessment. Such operationalised ideas could set a framework for work with young people, in effect a policy statement which could guide decision making, assessment and resourcing. The principles would or could be used to focus the use of resources by solving problems in context. These considerations could then involve a discussion of the young person's competences and difficulties, and the related contexts, together with steps taken (and proposed) to help. This would also help to develop a joint communication system and language, in addition it would assess what was to be done by whom, and what resources would be required.

In the process of assessment, aspects of previous models will remain useful: evaluative; best fit; placement; needs; may all have a place *if* they are considered with due regard to agreed principles or rights. The evaluative dimension, while not the only consideration must remain a central consideration, particularly in the development of principles or generally agreed rights.

Assessing assessment

Quite apart from polemic, belief and value bias, how is one to judge between different forms of assessment? To some extent this may be seen as a political, ethical, or professional issue, but the concept of outcomes and the evaluation of outcomes still figure as important factors. If assessment is to be based on hypothesis testing and problem solving, then evaluation and data gathering must be built in to help guide accurate assessment, placement and decision making.

One might reasonably expect the pragmatic best fit for the placement model, and the needs model to have been well versed in evaluation. What evidence has there been that children with identified need 'A' do better in placement 'X' rather than 'Y'? Do we gather evidence to make these decisions and to guide future decisions? Once more, literature searches (by Galloway and Goodwin (1987), Graham (1988), Johnstone and Munn (1987), H.M.I. (Choosing with Care) (1990)) have found little evidence of evaluation of these processes. The scant evidence available indicates little evaluation of assessment and placement processes and if anything provides evidence that the needs model may hinder integration (Dessent 1988, Solity 1991).

Assessment is often carried out in the context of decision making, and here the outcome can be seen to be influenced by the length and number of reports, and the extent of coverage of particular issues. Tutt (1984) has shown that large and more detailed reports are more likely to result in high tariff placement decisions regardless of actual content. This has also been supported by Tomlinson (1982). This may be because assessments were set to look at background and need for treatment, and to search for reasons and causes rather than focus on the presenting problems in relation to principles of practice and resources.

It seems evident that all levels of assessment depend upon feedback of data regarding success of outcome. If this is true of individual assessment then it must also be true of assessment as a process. The formulation of rights and principles could only be safety negotiated in the light of such findings. There is little point in setting up a particular statement as a right if it can be demonstrated not to be in the young persons best interests in terms of outcome. The use of data to assess assessment on specific criteria could also set the agenda for the assessment process, and the parameters of multi- disciplinary working (Gill and Pickles 1989).

An emerging consensus

The arguments proposed by McGuckin (1983) remain potent. High quality assessment and identification processes cannot be seen as isolated from the process of helping and working in difficult situations, neither can they be isolated from appropriate resourcing, interaction and outcomes. Developing ideas about assessment indicate that the process must involve a number of elements or features including; hypothesis testing, problem solving, evaluation, the inclusion of context, mutual power sharing, agreed language, open processes, and mutually understandable methods. It may be that the time spent on developing agreed principles or rights would help agreed action in many or all of these areas.

It is depressing to note that many of the papers quoted on assessment, covering many years, stress the idea of assessment as a process, while the notion of assessment as an activity which is done to/with a young person remains. If the elements necessary in an assessment process (see paragraph above) were present then this process would dictate appropriate methods, and more particularly methods which do not meet these criteria. The easy option of child centred deficit assessment can only be addressed if the value system is agreed, and if the process is influenced by evaluation and feedback of data.

The emerging rights/principles model of assessment ignores the importance of evaluation at its peril. The consensus evident in some authorities *is* the result of agreed principles (Allen, 1989). It seems clear that intellectual debate or polemic will convince few of the sceptics in the way which might be possible given specific principles allied to evaluated data. 'We should be open to changing our minds and the work's direction, the time for professional posing has long since gone' (McGuckin 1983).

Chapter 1

A progressive assessment framework can only be developed with regard to effective communication, agreed policies and resource allocation, in the context of articulated rights or principles. The title of this paper posed a question, what is the problem? The problem is the process of assessment and that is where we must seek solutions.

References

Allen, M & Fearon, B (1989). Central Region: A policy led youth strategy. In Gill, G & Pickles, T (1989).

Dessent, T (1988). Educational psychologists and the resource issue. In Jones and Sayer (1988).

Draper J, Fraser, H and Taylor, W (1982). *Working Together on Assessment.* T.A.I.P.S. Moray House.

Feiler, A (1988). The end of traditional assessment. In Thomas, G & Feiler, A (1988) *Planning for Special Educational Needs,* Blackwell.

Fisher, J (1978). Does anything work? *Journal of Social Service Research* V1(3).

Freiderickson, N, Webster, A, Wright, A (1991). *Psychological Assessment: A Change of Emphasis.* Educational Psychology in Practice V7 1.

Frude, N & Gault, H (1984). *Disruptive Behaviour in School.* Wiley.

Galloway, D (1985). *Schools, Pupils and Special Educational Needs.* Croom Helm, London.

Galloway, D & Goodwin, C (1987). *The Education of Disturbing Children.* Longman.

Gill, K & Pickles, T (1989). *Active Collaboration.* Glasgow I.T.R.C.

Gillham, B (1978). *Reconstructing Educational Psychology.* Croom Helm, London

Graham, J (1988). *Schools, Disruptive Behaviour and Delinquency.* H.M.S.O.

H.M. Inspectorate (1990). *Choosing with Care: The Provision of Pupils with Behavioural, Emotional and Social Difficulties.*

Hoghughi, M (1980). *Assessing Problem Children.* Andre Deutch.

Houston, J (1987). *Placing Girls in List D Schools.* R.P.S./S.E.D. 1986/7.

Jeffries, E (1990). The role of the specialist psychologist in work with under fives. *Support for Learning.* V5 2.

Johnstone, M & Munn, P (1987). *Discipline in Schools.* S.C.R.E.

Jones, N & Sayer, J (1988). *Management and the Psychology of Schooling.* The Falmer Press.

Kirkcaldy, B (1990). Special Education: towards a question of civil rights. *The Psychologist*, October 1990.

MacPhee, H (1987). *Exclusions: disturbing children in a disturbing situation.* S.E.D./R.P.S.

Maliphant, R (1974). Testing, testing? or will it be fine tomorrow. *Bulletin of B.P.S.* 27.

McGuckin, B (1983). Is assessment a dirty word? Unpublished paper, Central Region.

McLean, A (1987). After the belt, school processes in low exclusion schools. *School Organisation*, 19.

McManus, M (1980). *Troublesome Behaviour in the Classroom.* Routledge Education.

Pickles, T (1989). The implications of Active Collaboration. In Gill, H & Pickles, T. *Active Collaboration.* ITRC.

Reynolds, D & Sullivan, M (1981). 'The effects of school: a radical faith restated. In Gillham, B (1978).

Sayer, J (1983). Assessments for all, statements or none? *Special Education: Forward Trends*, 10, 15-16.

Solity, J (1991). Systematic assessment and teaching. In Jones, N & Sayer, J (1988).

Swanson, W I (1984). *The Assessment Procedures in the 1981 Act.* ITRC/Moray House.

Tattum, D (1978). *Disruptive Pupils in Schools and Units.* Wiley.

Tizard, B (1990). Research and policy: is there a link? *The Psychologist*, October 1990.

Tomlinson, S (1982). *The Sociology of Special Education.* Routledge and Kegan Paul, London.

Topping, K (1983). *Educational Systems for Disruptive Adolescents.* Croom Helm, London.

Trump, L (1991). The U.N. Convention on Human Rights - progress or fallacy? *Educational Psychology in Practice.* Volume 7, no. 2.

Tutt, (1984). *The Unintended Consequences of Integration.* ITRC/Moray House.

Wilson, M (1991). Assessing assessment. *Scottish Child,* July 1991.

Wilson, H (1984). *Who Decides? Procedures of Referral and Placement.* Jordanhill College.

Chapter 2

A Staff Development Approach to Improving Behaviour in Schools

Alan McLean

Introduction

Although there is no clear evidence to suggest a significant deterioration in childrens' behaviour, concern about it has been one of the most frequently reported sources of anxiety in most recent studies into teacher stress (Dunham 1985). Not surprisingly handling behaviour problems is among the most requested topics from teachers for in-service training. The Committee of Enquiry into Discipline in Schools in England and Wales (The Elton Report 1989) concluded their investigation by stating:

> '..the central problem of disruption could be significantly reduced by helping teachers to become more effective classroom managers ... and ... in-service training should include specific practical courses in ways of motivating and managing groups of pupils.'

The main sector of the education system in Scotland charged with the task of advising on problem behaviour is the psychological service. The traditional child centred approach taken by psychologists however focuses on childrens' personality and family background. The relevance of this approach has increasingly been questioned because it concentrates on elements which schools are least able to influence. This approach also involves assessing a child's difficulties in isolation from his relationship with his teachers and peers and so fails to take into account the teachers' style of pupil management and the curriculum on offer. Consequently advice from psychologists has often disappointed teachers because of its perceived lack of relevance and practicality. As effective pupil management involves continual decision making which needs to take into account a complex array of situational variables, prescriptive advice concerning particular children will always be of limited value. A more effective approach may be to seek improvement through developing teachers' understanding of school and classroom processes.

The Scottish Education Department Committee of Inquiry into Truancy and Indiscipline (known as the Pack Report) in 1977 was critical of the limited impact of the psychological service upon the problems of truancy and indiscipline. While the committee acknowledged the need for psychologists to have direct contact with individual children in order to be aware of their problems, it strongly recommended that the psychological service limit this role and concentrate on work with groups of parents and teachers. Since then psychologists themselves have reappraised their role (Gillham 1979) and sought to promote ways of collaborating with teachers which involve an examination of the processes of schooling as part of any explanation and management of problem behaviour.

This paper describes two such attempts in the form of training programmes devised by Strathclyde Psychological Service which attempts to provide a conceptual framework of pupil management from which teachers can make better informed decisions about their everyday teaching. 'Promoting Positive Behaviour in the Secondary School' is a course designed for secondary schools and 'Promoting Positive Behaviour in the Primary School' is the primary equivalent. This paper discusses the rationale behind the courses, their content, structure and methods of delivery.

These programmes aim to provide a stimulus and structure to enable teachers to address the issues related to children's behaviour in schools. They aim to facilitate a process of self directed professional development within a context of peer group support. The programmes are not ends in themselves but are best used to identify areas for further development at both the individual teacher and school levels. Promoted members of staff have an important role to play in providing follow up support.

Rationale

In relation to classroom management, teachers have traditionally been restricted in their ability to share their extensive knowledge and experience (Hargreaves 1980). The staff of a typical secondary school will collectively hold several centuries of experience in dealing with behaviour problems. Teachers as a group know not only more than anyone else about dealing with childrens' behaviour, they also know more than they realise. There are many reasons for this. Perhaps the main reasons include false assumptions about teaching being an intuitive skill and a natural gift solely reliant upon the 'right' personality. Much of the knowledge of successful teaching has been tacit knowledge which has not been easily put into words. In addition teachers have been reluctant to admit to problems in this area as this can be seen to imply incompetence. Another dimension of the problem is the traditional autonomy of teachers, the tendency to work alone, carefully protected from observation by colleagues. Furthermore there has been little feedback or self evaluation on professional competence in classroom discipline where the criteria of success or failure has been diffuse and intangible. There has always been a great deal of discussion in staffrooms about difficult pupils and their behaviour but little admission of teachers' real concerns and no real opportunity to properly discuss discipline issues or to challenge existing attitudes practices and policies.

Thus the skills of dealing with problem behaviour have often remained unspoken and unshared and any advice given to new teachers has tended to be unsystematic and contradictory. Consequently induction of new teachers in pupil management has been limited and teachers with 'discipline' problems have often been abandoned without support from senior colleagues.

Research findings from educational psychology have traditionally been considered irrelevant or impractical and have as such rarely found their way into schools. This research ignored the tacit knowledge of teachers and used instead the language and ideas of psychology. Teachers however have tended to reject these psychological formulations as alien. The lack of a conceptually refined language of classroom management has further restricted communication within the teaching profession. As a result the problems of low level but constant misbehaviour continue to be a great source of anxiety and frustration among both new and experienced teachers.

Research in the past fifteen years has improved this situation considerably by illuminating how successful teachers manage their classrooms (Evertson 1984, Kounin 1970, Hargreaves 1975, Kyriacou 1986, Wragg 1984). Teachers and pupils have been closely studied and teacher behaviours and school processes related to good pupil behaviour have been identified and described. This research evidence identifies effective practice and school processes which belong to and were created by teachers. This body of knowledge is not therefore new or unconventional. It is systematic common sense which provides a coherent conceptualisation of skills around which teachers can further develop their own practice. It offers easily understood knowledge which is directly related to the problems and issues of the school setting, and is familiar in terms of practical activities. Both programmes blend this research evidence with the most important resource - the collective experience and expertise of participants.

Disruption is demanding and immediate and requires interpretation and control. Being able to step back, reflect and take a more detached perspective has been found helpful in managing the problems as well as reducing the associated stress and exhaustion. This approach reinforces the growing trend among teachers to work together to manage their problems. This trend is reflected in the developments in co-operative and support teaching, discipline surgeries and case conferences, and multi-disciplinary school assessment groups.

Both programmes are essentially school and teacher centred. They examine preventive as opposed to reactive approaches. Few differences have been observed between schools and teachers in handling problems, but effective schools and teachers have been found to be skilled at preventing problems. The approach is positive and optimistic with the emphasis on the hidden curriculum. Continual reforms of the formal curriculum appear to have made little impact on childrens'

Chapter 2

behaviour and have overshadowed the importance of the informal curriculum. Concern with both aspects of school life is essential to achieve the most beneficial results.

The programmes are based on three key assumptions, namely:
1. Class teachers have the central responsibility for their own classroom discipline.
2. Teacher behaviour has a large influence on their pupils' behaviour.
3. Positive group management skills can be described, practised and acquired.

Structure

Both courses consist of twelve units designed for use in planned activity sessions or in-service days. Group leaders' guides provide suggestions for each activity along with activity and information papers. In addition each unit offers follow up ideas. A group leader is required to co-ordinate the programme, prepare the materials and organise the group exercises. The suggested timings and groupings are based on one group leader working with a group of about twelve during a 90 minute session. These arrangements should be adapted to suit other circumstances, for example two leaders, larger groups or longer sessions. The twelve units could be worked through in a series of clusters over a long term period. Most of the units however will stand alone and can be used in one-off sessions. A short course can be readily designed using a selection of elements from each of the units. The focus of such a course should be determined by the issues which are of greatest priority and concern to the staff. This has been found to be a very effective way of designing a successful course - determine what are the key issues in the school and create a course which looks at these issues from the different perspectives offered by relevant units. The leaders' instructions should be seen as suggestions rather than prescriptions and courses will be of most benefit to staff if they are adapted to meet their particular needs.

Training Videos

Each programme has its own accompanying training video the purpose of which is to stimulate discussion and encourage teachers within a humorous and non-threatening context to identify with the teachers in the video and acknowledge their own strengths and weaknesses. The scenes were enacted by the teachers and pupils through role play and improvisation around loosely pre-determined scenarios. Mostly the scenarios are given in pairs to provide contrasting situations or more effective or less effective practice illustrating different aspects of class management. The scenes can readily be contextualised to provide a focus upon particular issues.

Chapter 2

Summary of Content

School Ethos

The aim of this unit is to discuss and share participants' ideas about the concept of ethos and to then evaluate the ethos in their own school. Recent research findings clearly show that schools vary markedly with respect to their pupils' behaviour and that these differences are independent of intake (Rutter 1979, Mortimore 1988).

These variations are strongly associated with the characteristics of schools as social institutions and there is some evidence that certain aspects of a school's ethos are associated with and lead to good pupil outcomes. Among the issues which this unit looks at are the following:

    i.   What do you understand by the term 'ethos'?
    ii.   Who or what are the main determinants of the ethos in the school?
    iii. How is the school ethos communicated to staff, pupils and parents?
    iv. Does the school have a shared ethos which transmits its main values?
    v.   How does the school support teachers in maintaining good behaviour?

Rules

This unit reviews the qualities of successful rules and attempts to determine criteria for effective rules. Groups tend to arrive at a similar set of rules about rules, eg. they should be few and positive. These seem self evident but when they are applied to the school or class rules there is often a major discrepancy. This unit asks some searching questions:

    i.   Should all teachers have the same class rules?
    ii.   Do all teachers consistently enforce the school rules?
    iii. If all teachers in the same school share a 'core' set of rules what are they?
    iv. Are there any school rules which some teachers particularly dislike - why?
    v.   How could schools involve parents in creating the school rules?

The unit then goes on to establish how children know how to behave - how do they find out about the rules - how do the teachers communicate the rules to them? Again this is taken for granted but it has been found useful to look at imaginative ways of communicating rules in the classroom, for example using a thematic approach for particularly difficult groups. One interesting approach was put forward by a participant where a group of children were not complying with the 'stay in seat' rule. The teacher set up an air traffic control project where the children had to pretend to fasten their seat belts and receive permission from air traffic control to leave their seats. This captured the childrens' imagination and helped establish this basic classroom rule.

Minimising Dead Time

'Dead time' occurs whenever no teaching or learning is taking place; the more dead time the more disruption. In particular the most common and frustrating cause of 'dead time' appears to be interruptions to classroom momentum. The programmes focus on this theme of 'dead time' created by interruptions in the classroom. Despite the widespread view among teachers of its importance in causing disruption, there has been little evidence found of school policies on classroom interruptions.

Another recurring issue concerns 'dead time' where a child does nothing for long periods of time. Useful strategies to monitor and minimize individual pupil 'dead time' have emerged. For example a simple grid on the teacher's desk which allows children with this tendency to record their progress every time they complete a task is an effective monitoring system which keeps the pupils accountable.

Disruptive transitions from one activity to another is a further common source of 'dead time' (Kounin 1970). For example when the teacher has to repeat instructions or refer back to omitted instructions or when new instructions contradict earlier instructions. An essential element in smooth transitions is clear switch signalling by which the teacher tells the pupils explicitly that the activities are changing and implicitly that the rules are changing. This concept is more readily understood by secondary teachers with the more clearly differentiated phases to their lessons. However the concept is equally relevant and important in primary schools.

Picking Up Signals

This unit identifies the key aspects of teacher behaviour which convey awareness. An appropriate image might be one given by one participant in a particular course of '...a teacher going around the class on a skateboard with wing mirrors on her shoulders!' Pupil comments such as 'you must have eyes in the back of your head' are indicators of a teacher with good skills in picking up signals, particularly early warning signals of pupil unrest or distress. The key elements include the following:

good positioning of teacher and pupils for maximum visibility,
regular scanning of the whole room,
good overlapping; that is doing more than one thing at a time,
picking up early warning signs of pupil inattention,
stopping misbehaviour early with a brief light 'attention grabber'.

Ignoring misbehaviour is a subtle and often misunderstood but effective strategy. The skill is knowing when to turn a blind eye. The experienced teacher does so when:

A) the behaviour is
minor or momentary attention-seeking,
isolated to one pupil,
a 'one off' for the pupil,
not endangering others or self,
not challenging the teacher's authority, or when

B) the child
has been set up by peers,
can change his own behaviour given time.

To reprimand in any of these occasions would only disrupt the class, give attention to the attention seeker, provoke a confrontation or collude with peer victimisation. Ignoring is most effective when it is immediately followed by giving praise to a child behaving appropriately. In this way the teacher lets the child know without any fuss that he has been spotted.

Conveying Authority

This unit identifies the key aspects of teacher behaviour which convey status and authority (Robertson 1981). This is the area where the lack of teacher exchange of knowledge is most apparent; teacher authority is considered by most an enigma or a game of bluff. Not surprisingly this is the area found most useful by new teachers, particularly those who have not yet managed to 'crack the secret code'. It is also the area where many teachers with discipline problems have the greatest difficulties and receive the least support. This is probably because colleagues will have found it difficult to give them feedback without fear of offending them. Criticism of the teacher in this area sails very close to criticising the teacher as a person. For these reasons some teachers with difficulties in this aspect of the job have gone without support and have had to develop maladaptive self defence mechanisms.

How to establish your authority does not need to be a mystery and the blend of research evidence together with a group's pooled experience provides a structure in which to understand the dynamics involved. Some important authority conveying behaviour includes:

i. asserting your own authority rather than referring to a higher authority,
ii. entering pupils' territory as opposed to being static,
iii. setting your agenda rather than allowing the pupils to set their agenda,
iv. gaining silence before speaking instead of competing with the noise,
v. presenting appropriate body language and a quietly spoken voice.

A loud shrill voice communicates clearly to children that the teacher is struggling to establish authority.

Classroom Climate

This unit looks at the ways in which classroom climates are created and communicated. The learning environment in each classroom is determined by the tone or atmosphere permeating the classroom. Just as the class teacher has to be responsible for clearly setting his own agenda and set of rules in order to establish his authority he must also set the climate in his room. The teacher's attitude and expectations are central to this. Research evidence suggests that teachers effective in creating positive climates share the following features (Hargreaves 1975):

> they show high self-esteem; foster positive attitudes to learning; nurture pupil self-esteem; make pupils feel capable, significant, involved; use a lot of praise to build rapport; try not to stereotype pupils; don't jump to conclusions; fairly distribute attention and praise; adopt a participative rather than coercive approach.

Research has shown how teachers tend to perceive boys and girls as discrete groups, especially male teachers (Stanworth 1981). Primary teachers seem to prefer teaching girls, while their colleagues in secondary schools prefer teaching boys. There is however no suggestion that teachers are biased towards pupils of their own sex. Boys have been found to dominate classrooms in areas crucial for self-esteem, namely teacher attention, concern, praise and questioning. At the same time teachers also criticise boys more often and more harshly. Girls are further treated differently in that for them school rule breaking is fused with gender rule breaking. For example, girls who break a school rule by arguing with a teacher are also seen to break one of society's rules about female behaviour. Over time girls tend to become less involved in the classroom and this appears to be acceptable to teachers. Clearly teachers are not solely responsible for any gender divisions in their classrooms as pupils also interact on the basis of gender. However, teachers who are aware of the pattern of interactions in their classrooms which reinforce gender divisions can try to create a climate in which girls can more readily participate.

Stopping Misbehaviour

The purpose of this unit is to evaluate the effectiveness of different styles of interventions aimed at stopping misbehaviour. A reprimand should be distinguished from a punishment which aims to avoid the behaviour recurring. Some teachers often give ineffective reprimands because they confuse reprimands with punishments and consequently over-reprimand. The confusion can sometimes come about because the teacher is so frustrated with the behaviour that he wants some form of retribution or revenge.

This unit tries to do two things. It stresses the fact that although teachers may be limited by the range of reprimands they are less restricted in their style of reprimand. Secondly, it tries to challenge assumptions such as loud and public reprimands are more effective than quiet and private reprimands. This is one of the few areas where research evidence does not coincide with many experienced teachers' views. Anyone watching more than a few scenes from the videos will be struck by the fundamental importance of the voice, its tone, pitch and volume in signalling to pupils the emotional state of their teacher. The voice is central to pupil management, and reprimanding is a key classroom interaction skill for teachers.

Reward Styles

Different reward styles are reviewed and the key aspects of teacher behaviours which motivate children are identified. The power of the positive approach is emphasised in this unit (Cheeseman and Watts 1985, Clarizio 1980, Wheldall 1987). For whatever reason many teaches become sceptical about the principles inherent in behavioural psychology. They need to be persuaded about the well documented advantages of rewards in promoting a positive self image, a positive attitude towards the teacher and subject, and a longer lasting effect on behaviour. Rewards teach what to do as well as what not to do, result in the child behaving when the teacher is not there and are useful in assessing how much control the child has over his behaviour.

Rewards of course can sometimes carry 'hidden punishments'. A reward is something that follows a behaviour and causes it to happen more often; if the behaviour does not happen more often then it cannot be a reward. Most teachers have experienced the frustration of trying to reward children only to discover they were unwittingly punishing them!

Clearly there are reservations among teachers about using rewards in the classroom which need to be addressed. These include:

i. giving children rewards is a form of bribery;
ii. the more rewards you give, the more they will demand;
iii. if you give rewards you will be seen as a 'soft touch';
iv. if you give a special reward to one child, everyone will want one.

Many teachers are reluctant to reward problem pupils for behaviour which is normally taken for granted. Schools are rewarding to most pupils, but mainly in terms of achievement. Troubled children do not experience many of these intrinsic naturally occurring rewards. This is why these children need incentives for expected behaviour. These rewards need to be extrinsic, that is not directly related to the task, to motivate the children until they can naturally access the intrinsic rewards.

Group Behaviour Strategies

This unit describes and evaluates a variety of strategies designed to improve the behaviour of difficult groups or classes, the majority of which use some form of reward system. These strategies have to be practical, quick, easy to operate and simple to monitor. In addition they must be compatible with class organisation. Ideally they should provide a visual display of progress, set clear criteria for good behaviour and harness peer group pressure appropriately. These appear to be the features which will most likely lead to teachers using them and pupils responding to them.

One of the most effective and simplest systems to emerge involves the teacher giving every child in the class four markers at the start of the day. Each time a child produces the target behaviour, for example shouting out and being overheard by the teacher above the general noise of the class a card is taken from him. Eight cards are exchanged for thirty minutes of activities at the end of the day twice in the week. This strategy like the others is very effective in settling a particularly unruly group or class.

Individual Behaviour Strategies

This unit argues for the use of behaviour charts as an effective strategy for changing problem behaviour of individual children. It is crucial that any chart targets one specific discrete behaviour which will be possible to change and will hopefully prevent other more serious problems. In addition it is vital that the behaviour is observable and measurable so that specific limits can be set. If an appropriate behaviour is selected, behaviour charts can be very effective. They work for good reasons including:

1. the child knows exactly what he is required to do from the clear consistent and objective feedback;
2. the child obtains a clear visual display of progress towards targets which are manageable because they are broken down into small steps and units of time.

This is in stark contrast to most behaviour monitoring systems in schools, particularly secondary schools which expect the pupil to be well behaved in every aspect of behaviour, in every setting, all of the time, for a whole week! A common reason for charts not working is that the teacher fails to keep to the agreement. For example teachers withdrawing the reward, despite the child having earned it, because he has misbehaved in some other way. Their mistake is to fail to realise that the normal discipline procedures should be maintained while a child is on a behaviour chart.

Behaviour charts have some advantageous 'side effects'. For example they are particularly helpful in breaking the negative teacher/pupil interaction freeing the teacher to take a more positive approach to the pupil; they focus the teacher's attention on priority behaviour and provide a consistent framework for responding to the child.

Punishments

This unit reviews the most effective use of sanctions which have a central part to play in promoting positive behaviour if used effectively. The most common and recurring reason why many punishments imposed on children are ineffective and the children continue to repeat the misbehaviour is that the punishments are not punishing. Indeed many teacher punishments are rewarding and can encourage the misbehaviour to be repeated! (Cheeseman and Watts 1985)

This is most evident in the common mis-use of 'time out'. The aim is often to remove the child so that he won't disrupt but if being placed in 'time out' is more rewarding than the classroom, certain pupils will increase their misbehaviour to be placed there. 'Time out' should be preceded by a warning. The unwanted behaviour should always be clearly stated along with the appropriate behaviour. The child should be removed expediently and calmly for a period which should be short, from 2 to 10 minutes to an unrewarding environment.

Confrontations

This unit aims to review and extend participants' options for defusing confrontations. Many teaches restrict themselves to a limited repertoire of coping strategies and the objective is to find particular strategies which fit the teacher's own personality. Some examples from the 'Options for defusing confrontations' checklist include:

1. **Maintain rapport** by calming the pupil's emotions through mood matching, pacing and leading; use tension releasers, eg. unfolding arms, taking off jacket, gentle forward movement; tilting back chair.

2. **Stay in control** by responding rather than reacting; not jumping to conclusions; monitoring your own feelings; controlling your voice tone, volume and gestures.

3. **Try not to stir it up** by dealing only with the immediate issue; not bringing up the past or personalizing the issue.

4. **Avoid dead ends** by not getting into power struggles; not asking why or demanding an admission of guilt.

5. **Keep an escape route open** by leaving yourself and the child a face saving way out; offering a cooling off period; giving pupil manageable steps to regain self control.

Defusing confrontations may not always be the answer. Many teachers particularly in the primary sector prefer to confront the child and work through the problem. But when is it appropriate to confront a child? What does the teacher need to consider beforehand? Before the teacher decides to escalate a confrontation, she certainly needs to consider two issues. Firstly, what are the pupil's motives for provoking the confrontation? It is helpful for the teacher to consider how the child's behaviour makes her feel as a clue to the child's aims and motive. For example, if the teacher feels annoyed, the child is probably trying to 'wind her up' with an attention seeking motive. If on the other hand the teacher feels outraged, the child's motive is more likely to be revenge. Secondly, are there any mechanisms for accessing immediate support? Some unobtrusive but effective systems have been described by participants which allow the teacher to access immediate support from a colleague. In one example, if a child was thought to be going out of control, the teacher would send a child to the colleague with the class list. The list would have a red asterisk beside the troubled child's name. The

Chapter 2

supporting colleague would quickly come into the class and quietly distract the pupil and defuse the potentially explosive situation.

Implementation

In both the primary and secondary sector it is essential for the programme to carry status within the school with the headteacher seen to support the programme. Both programmes are most effectively held in participants' own schools. Joint group leaders have been found to be very effective, and adequate time and resources, for planning and preparation, have to be given to the group leaders.

Running a course in a primary school is more straightforward than in a secondary as the smaller size allows the whole staff group to be involved. *In the secondary school, implementation should be considered as a long term goal and the programme should be phased in gradually with staged objectives. The goal should be to 'institutionalise' the programme in the sense of making it an integral pat of the annual whole school programme. The eventual involvement of every member of staff need not be considered a realistic or desirable aim. Implementation should start in a small way, with for example a short and carefully designed pilot course. A steering group is useful to support the designated group leader(s). The first group of teachers should be carefully selected to include some teachers who have a well recognised ability in this area in order to avoid any sense of stigma. For the same reason teachers with highly visible discipline problems should never be grouped together for special attention.*

No one format of time allocation has been found to be most effective. Alternative models tried and found useful have included timetabled meetings, departmental meetings, one off seminars, part of a review of school discipline, a series of planned activity times or half day in-service sessions. *Participation should always be voluntary.* The time scale of any course should be determined by the aims of the particular course, the group composition, its format and structure as well as on any school based restrictions. A comprehensive course for new teachers might for example consist of fortnightly one hour meetings throughout the whole session. A refresher course for experienced staff might on the other hand consist of six sessions.

The most effective size of group has been found to be between six and ten. Any group should consist ideally of teachers with varying lengths of experience, with different levels of expertise and from a mixture of departments.

Alternative Uses

These materials have been used for purposes other than staff development courses. They have been used for private study for example, although this precludes the vital element of exchange of ideas. They have provided the focus for an informal 'support group' of interested teachers in one school. They have provided material which was used as a method of self or peer evaluation. Some teachers in management positions have found them helpful in providing structured feedback to colleagues regarding particular class management difficulties. This allows a constructive focus on specific behaviours rather than on the teacher as a person. Some schools have used the programme to hold a discipline audit or review.

Some of the recently emerging behaviour support services are beginning to use the materials to offer courses as one element of their response to requests from school for help. In addition, the framework provided by the programmes has potential for offering an interactive structure with which to analyse childrens' behavioural difficulties and identify changes in how staff handle the child. Such an assessment checklist would ask, for example - with which particular rules does the child have difficulty complying? - to which form of reprimand does the child best respond?

Although the programmes were designed primarily for use in mainstream primary and secondary schools, the universal principles of child and group management will be relevant in day and residential special schools, nursery schools and further education colleges. A training video has been made for a further education version of Preventing Disruption - 'Issues in Classroom Management in F.E.' (CAST 1991). The materials are beginning to be used in pre-service teacher training courses, although the lack of on-going experience and ready opportunity to experiment with alternative strategies are likely to limit their value to pre-service students.

Potential Pitfalls

Working with any group of professional staff on such a sensitive issue as the discipline of children comes with potential hazards some of which include:

> The programme can be a vehicle or focus for underlying tensions within the staff group;
>
> The senior staff can become threatened by the issues raised and consequently become defensive;
>
> Staff with major difficulties in managing behaviour can become further demoralised and isolated unless their concerns are sensitively followed up;
>
> The programme can be 'hijacked' by dominant personalities who seek to follow their own agendas and assert their own points of view;

Some teachers will insist upon answers on how to solve the problems of children with extreme behaviour problems;

External group leaders can unwittingly be placed in a difficult situation by headteachers who have a different perception of staff needs to that of the staff.

Conclusion

The best way to avoid these problems is to stress positively but sensitively the aims and assumptions of the programmes and so clarify expectations at the outset. If the course has a mechanism for conveying outcomes to senior management, it will be seen positively as a method of empowering class teachers to communicate their views about aspects of school and classroom practice and policy. The key selling point is that the programmes are about how teachers can provide mutual support by sharing their ideas on how to prevent or reduce the main behaviour problems that beset teachers, that is low level but continual misbehaviour. It is not the intention of the programmes to provide a set of prescriptions for success or instant solution to all behaviour problems. They are not offering expert advice, blaming teachers or telling them how to do their job.

Participants are asked to analyse their own policies and practices using a rational set of principles, and then to act upon their analyses. There is a tendency to expect neat and packaged solutions from experts, but such a search grounded in desperation leads only to grasping at straws. Energy and positive attitudes can replace exhaustion and disillusion only if a positive approach is adopted in which teachers perceive the management of pupils' behaviour as an issue about which everyone has something to learn and something to give.

Copies of the programme are available from:

Sales & Publications
Jordanhill College of Education
76 Southbrae Drive
Glasgow G13 1PP
Tel. 041-950 3170/3171

References

Bull, S and Solity, J (1987). *Classroom Managemen*. Croom Helm.

Charlton, T and David, K (eds) (1989). *Managing Misbehaviour*. Macmillan Education.

Cheeseman, P and Watts, P (1985). *Positive Behaviour Management: A Manual for Teachers*. Croom Helm.

Clarizio, H (1980). *Towards Positive Classroom Discipline*. John Wiley.

Cohen, L and Cohen, A (eds) (1987). *Disruptive Behaviour; A Source Book for Teachers*. Harper and Row.

Department of Education (1989). The Committee of Enquiry into Discipline in Schools in England and Wales (The Elton Report).

Docking, J (1980). *Control and Discipline in Schools*. Harper & Row.

Dunham, J (1985). *Teacher Stress*. Croom Helm.

Frude, N and Gault, H (eds) (1984). *Disruptive Behaviour in Schools*. John Wiley.

Galloway, D and Goodwin, C (1987). *The Education of Disturbing Children*. Longman.

Gillham, W (1979). *Reconstructing Educational Psychology*. Croom Helm.

Hargreaves, D (1975). *Deviance in Classrooms*. Routledge and Kegan Paul.

Hargreaves, D (1980). Teachers' knowledge of behaviour problems. In Upton and Gobell *Behaviour Problems in Schools*. University College, Cardiff.

Kounin, J (1970). *Discipline and Group Management in Classrooms*. Holt Rinehart and Winston.

Kyriacou, C (1986). *Effective Teaching in Schools*. Basil Blackwell.

Laslett, R and Smith C (1984). *Effective Classroom Management*. Croom Helm.

Montgomery, D (1989). *Managing Behaviour Problems*. Hodder and Stoughton.

Mortimore, P et al (1988). *School Matters: The Junior Years.* Open Books.

Reid, K, Hopkins, D and Holly, P (1987). *Towards the Effective School.* Basil Blackwell.

Roberts, T (1983). *Child Management in the Primary School.* George Allen and Unwin.

Robertson, J (1981). *Effective Classroom Control.* Hodder and Stoughton.

Rutter, M et al (1979). *Fifteen Thousand Hours: Secondary Schools and their Effects on Pupils.* Open Books.

Stanworth, M (1981). *Gender and Schooling.* Hutchinson.

Tattum, D (ed) (1986). *Management of Disruptive Pupil Behaviour in Schools.* John Wiley and Sons.

Watkins, C and Wagner, P (1987). *School Discipline: A Whole School Approach.* Basil Blackwell.

Wheldall, K (ed) (1987). *The Behaviourist in the Classroom.* Allen and Unwin.

Chapter 3

Guidance
Sandy Peterson

Guidance was born in confusion, created by two different ideas. The desire to provide a helping service to pupils in large, impersonal schools was balanced against a desire to control increasingly difficult behaviour. Children, affected by the loosening of society's bonds, had seemingly lost their fear of adults in authority. Faced with growing indiscipline teachers had two choices. They could continue to enforce discipline by punitive methods, or find a new way of persuading pupils to behave in ways acceptable to schools and society. The debate between supporters of these two strategies has never been settled. Many teachers have maintained faith in their ability to exert authority, backed by institutional systems of referral, punishment and exclusion while others have experimented with a range of methods which shift responsibility for behaviour on to pupils. This may seem a healthy debate between professionals, but for pupils caught in the middle it has been confusing and even damaging. Intelligent, mature youngsters from settled homes have been able to pick their way through the contradictions, but damaged, insecure pupils have had their internal confusions compounded.

Pupils were not the only ones caught in the middle. Guidance teachers have also wandered in this no-mans-land. Their teacher training, their childhood experience and their loyalty to colleagues pulled them in one direction, while their intimate knowledge of pupils' lives and awareness of the inadequacy of traditional methods suggested a new direction. Guidance teachers recognize that schools prefer unquestioning acceptance of rules and procedures, and find it difficult to cater for the individual needs and desires of pupils - or staff. The greater involvement of parents and politicians in the affairs of schools has increased the pressure on teachers to enforce discipline. Both these groups have a simplistic view of education, based on myths about the 'good old days'. The direct effect of the Parents Charter has been to encourage schools with a traditional approach to behaviour, and discourage schools which have sought a more liberal, equal relationship with their pupils. Another result of all the contradictory pressures has been a confusion of guidance methods and approaches. Not only do different schools and different teachers work in incompatible ways, but the same guidance teacher often uses a range of methods which do not add up to a coherent whole.

Guidance staff, rationalizing to defend their practice, have even come to see variety as a virtue. Eclecticism and pragmatism are titles bestowed on confusion, in an attempt to justify an absence of coherent philosophy. I am not suggesting that any single method will meet all contingencies, but there must be a basic consistency of approach to all people in all situations. This will allow pupils, parents and other professionals to understand the purpose and function of guidance which needs to do now what it failed to do 20 years ago, namely work out its principles and practices, and find a theoretical foundation which will allow its teachers to withstand the assaults from the forces which have something to gain from 'capturing' guidance. Many guidance teachers seem reluctant to spend time working on philosophy. They assume that, because intentions are honourable, good results must follow. Lacking a specific guidance philosophy, most guidance staff simply take on, without thinking, the philosophy of the institution. I recently asked 40 guidance teachers, all of whom described themselves as child-centred, which strategies they used when dealing with difficult pupils. Of the 20 strategies described, 19 were strongly authoritarian and controlling, with the clear aim of persuading pupils to conform to school rules. The exception was that of counselling, but further investigation revealed a model which allowed little or no room for decision-making by pupils and in fact amounted to no more than advice-giving by the teachers. Without a basic philosophy, guidance practice will be a series of reactions to problems, always with the aim of helping the pupils, but without recognizable shape or direction.

The first step towards finding a philosophy is to decide who guidance is for. In my opening remarks I suggested that guidance was created to change the behaviour of pupils who fail to conform. If this seems simplistic I do not want to imply a lack of desire to care for all pupils. The problem arises from the naivety of the assumption that pupils' needs and the school's needs automatically coincide. I think this view still prevails in that most guidance proceeds on the basis that school knows what's best. Guidance teachers are preoccupied with persuading pupils of the advisability of accepting the school's view and interpretation of events. A guidance teacher's success is judged by managers, colleagues, parents and the public by the degree to which pupils adhere to institutional and social rules.

Consider, for example, a typical guidance dilemma. A pupil has been involved in a public dispute with a classroom teacher. The guidance teacher has been informed and has arranged an interview with the pupil. The A.H.T. has also received a report of the incident and will be expected to take disciplinary action. In most schools it is accepted that the guidance role differs from that of management. Put simply, the A.H.T. is expected to punish, and the guidance teacher is expected to do something else. But what? If the guidance teacher, having listened to the pupil decides that (s)he is in the right and takes the pupil's side, there is an automatic conflict with the A.H.T. This 'guidance versus discipline' tension is dealt with in two ways. In some schools such differences run like a poison through the system, creating tensions among staff and leaving pupils and parents in hopeless confusion; in other schools a strange compromise has emerged, which allows both 'discipliners' and 'guiders' to operate independently. Such an arrangement may seem to give guidance freedom and status but there is an alternative interpretation. By allowing guidance to operate, but denying it power, management can continue to impose the institutional will on pupils, while seeming to address pupils' needs. Guidance teachers who accept such a role are little more than collaborators, acting as advocates and apologists for the decisions of managers and subject teachers. I find it easy to understand a guidance teacher who wants to support the school and protect colleagues, but such a person has little to offer to pupils whose differing needs require the attention of a professional with an open mind and a willingness to fight for the rights of the individual.

It is only after clarification of a basic philosophy that a guidance teacher can select appropriate methods for working with pupils. Different events do require different reactions, but each method used must emanate from a recognizable set of principles. If, to continue the previous argument, we believe that young people should be told how to behave then we must choose methods to ensure that outcome. If, on the other hand, we believe that young people need to take responsibility for their own behaviour, then we should find strategies appropriate to that belief. Both these approaches are equally benevolent and equally concerned for children's welfare, but they diverge at a critical point in a child's development. The authoritarian guidance teacher and the democratic guidance teacher will deal similarly with the dependent 12 year old, but whereas the authoritarian is happy to retain that position throughout the school, the democrat wants the 16 year old child to be making real decisions and must engage in a lengthy process of moving the pupil towards independence.

I am a strong believer in the democratic approach but, over the last few years, my disputes have been, not with the unashamed authoritarians, but with those who preach democracy and practise control. Child-centredness is in fashion, and I'm glad of it, but it has acquired some comical converts. Attitudes change less quickly than jargon, and I'm not convinced by the recent guidance enthusiasm for less directive methods. There is much talk about pupils taking responsibility and making decisions, but there is little evidence of pupils having power over their own school lives. I am not suggesting that this apparent duplicity is caused by cynical manipulation of pupils by guidance teachers, but rather that it results from a failure to understand the implications of any philosophy. This uncertainty is demonstrated in the illogical choice and application of various methods, without checking if the likely outcome is desirable. With the benefit of 20 years' experience it is possible to calculate the likely consequence of the various strategies used in guidance. I want to look at several popular examples and attempt to do that calculation.

Chapter 3

Counselling

Most guidance teachers claim to use counselling in their work. There are many types of counselling, but a common fundamental principle is the right of the client to express thoughts and feelings and to take decisions about action to deal with problems. If we return to the pupil we mentioned earlier, who was reported for bad behaviour, and we decide to use a counselling approach then we must accept that the pupil can freely discuss all aspects and make decisions about future action. The guidance teacher's contribution to the interview will be very significant and challenging, but will not include making a decision about what is to happen. Experience suggests that most pupils will make acceptable decisions, but that cannot be guaranteed. Counselling cannot be used to persuade or enforce, and the counsellor must accept the client's decisions. Guidance teachers who counsel may thus have to accept anti-institutional decisions, but where does this leave the A.H.T. who is expected to enforce school policies? How does the classroom teacher feel, having been implicitly, if not explicitly, criticised?. Where, and this is most crucial, does this leave the pupil and the parent? The conclusion must be that counselling is inappropriate in a school run on purely authoritarian lines. It may be legitimate to have pupils describe incidents and discuss possible actions, but it needs to be clear from the start that the school will decide the outcome, with or without the pupil's agreement.

Is it possible to use counselling in schools? I believe it is, if certain conditions can be applied. The school must accept that pupils, by 4th year, have the same rights as teachers. In return pupils must agree that the school, in order to operate, needs rules and procedures which apply equally to all children and adults, and which would be established democratically. In such a situation counselling can take place between a teacher and pupil who have equal power, and who are both aware of the needs and rights of the institution. The guidance teacher can support the pupil's decisions because (s)he is not responsible for the consequences of that decision. Counselling can therefore take place, and be effective, but only with pupils who have achieved the necessary state of independence. This in turn means that counselling cannot be used as a method with children in primary schools or in early secondary, though there is an essential preparation phase during which relationships between teachers and pupils need to move from dependence towards independence. Freedom doesn't work if it comes too quickly. That fact has been proven in social history, and applies to adults as well as children. Younger pupils can be taught and encouraged to express feelings and explore consequences of actions without the pressure of having to make decisions before they are ready.

Once the school has accepted counselling in principle, there is also a requirement to prepare teachers and parents, whose expectations must move from an assumption that guidance will support their every action to a belief in the value of children making decisions, including 'bad' ones, and learning from the experience.

Behaviour Contracts

I mentioned earlier that I had asked a number of teachers about the methods used for dealing with difficult pupils. From their answers and my own observations I would be confident in stating that all Scottish secondary schools operate a version of the behaviour contract, behaviour check or behaviour timetable. Procedures vary a little, but the common purpose is close monitoring and control of behaviour, which is rewarded or punished according to performance. Parents are often involved and directly associated with the rewards and punishments.

Such methods have a diametrically opposite aim to counselling. They are based on a belief in the desirability of teacher control and are the logical application of an authoritarian system. It is often said in their defence that pupils like them, but such approval is possibly an indication of children's preference for the security of dependence. It is much easier to be told what to do, especially as there is the added advantage of having someone else to blame. There is no doubt that behaviour checks affect pupils' actions. Their weakness lies in their inability to stimulate independent thought and self-control.

Most contracts that I have seen derive more directly from the Mafia than the dictionary. There is a concentration on improved pupil behaviour, but no mention of teacher behaviour. The threats are clear, the consequences of failure are calamitous, but the rewards are often derisory. 'Change your attitude and behaviour and we'll give you something from the tuck shop and let you watch late night television.' No account is taken of reasons for disturbed behaviour, or the extreme difficulty any human has in changing fundamental patterns of behaviour. In short, a contract is not an agreement between free parties, but a set of conditions imposed by the school. My objection is not so much to the principle as to the basic dishonesty of the process. If we want to control children then let's say so.

It is understandable that guidance teachers, faced with varied problems, should want a range of methods. It is less easy to justify the confused manner in which contradictory strategies are applied in an apparently haphazard manner. It is possible for a pupil to be given a behaviour check at 9 am and to have a counselling session at 3 pm. At 9 am (s)he receives clear instructions about behaviour, while at 3 pm (s)he is given, apparently, the power to decide how to behave. Little wonder that the pupil is confused, and the guidance teacher seen as a feebly failed authoritarian.

I am not saying that counselling and behaviour control cannot co-exist in a school, but there must be logic in their use. The sight of a twelve year old with a 'behaviour card' does not upset me, but if (s)he's still carrying it as (s)he approaches 16 years old I shall want to ask why. We need a systematic approach to guidance, which recognizes our responsibility to move pupils from school control to self-control. At the moment there is no sign of such a child-control criterion in guidance. We judge guidance teachers on their pupil's adherence to school rules, as if that was enough.

Groupwork

Like counselling, groupwork has acquired magical powers in dealing with difficult behaviour. At Children's Hearings and case conferences the decision to place a child in a group is seen as automatically beneficial. I do not have the knowledge to do a critical analysis of groupwork methods, but I shall describe a style which I have observed several times. A group is set up to help pupils with behavioural difficulties. The aim of the group exercise is to change that difficult behaviour. It is my impression that in recent years the methods used have become more behavioural, targeting specific problems. Youngsters who are members of the group are encouraged to form close, friendly relationships with each other and with the adult leaders who are teachers, social workers, community workers, etc. The members are encouraged to express their thoughts and feelings and to become involved in planning the group's programme.

I attended a meeting of such a group recently. When I arrived the pupils were engaged in sports and activities. The atmosphere was pleasant, relationships were relaxed and any verbal or physical aggression was purely taken. I was made welcome by the young people who showed well-developed social skills which had probably been learned in the group. At an agreed time we had the group meeting, sitting around a table with tea and rolls. The purpose of the meeting was to recount the events of the past week and discuss any issues or problems which had arisen. The youngsters talked mainly about problems with their teachers, who were criticised and often derided. The adult leaders, who included a guidance teacher from the school, listened attentively, sometimes laughed along with the youngsters, and usually put across the teachers' and the school's point of view without always agreeing with it. Some group members contributed to the discussion, while others were restless and anxious to return to physical activity. The meeting concluded after some talk about future activities, trips and summer camp.

I am interested in what such sessions achieve. I strongly believe that young people benefit from such experiences. They learn skills, they form relationships and they deal with adults in a relaxed environment. I am, however, sceptical about the likelihood of direct effect on school or classroom behaviour. When I spoke to the A.H.T. responsible for making referrals to the group he said wryly that some pupils seemed to have got worse. Firstly, I think that is quite likely, and secondly it should be no surprise. Bringing together a number of difficult youngsters may simply lend group re-inforcement to anti-social behaviour. What is a gang, after all? Unless the adult leaders have the skill and knowledge to create, in the peer group, a positive force for change, then the naturally negative influence of the stronger youngsters will prevail. If a child criticises her teacher in the group meeting, receives jocular support from peers and tacit approval or muted argument from adults, then where is the challenge to change?

Groups can change behaviour for the better, but only if the leaders discover what motivates youngsters, and can provide a level of support which will sustain change. It is unlikely that any real good can come from groups which meet for a few hours every week, unless that session is a small part of a greater plan. This means that the method chosen in groupwork must dovetail with the guidance practice of the school, and the philosophy of management and teachers, not forgetting social work and other involved agencies. Once again the method must suit the purpose. The behavioural approaches which are currently popular make perfect sense if the purpose is to make the child behave in a way which is acceptable to an authoritarian school. Such a process should not allow free expression of grievances in a group setting, but would require the leaders to devise and impose a programme of specific rewards for specific improvements, and reject as pointless any discussion of the faults of the school. This group method has the same function as individual behaviour programmes and can be as successful, provided that its limitations are recognised. Short-term changes can be produced. In a special unit in which I worked, we practically eliminated lateness, truancy and failure to work. However the long-term effect may be to increase youngsters' dependence on adults, and to continue immature reactions to authority. In the same special unit we had little success in affecting attitudes, and we succeeded only when we became deeply involved in all aspects of a child's life at home, in the community and in the school. In groupwork, as in individual work, there may be a quick fix for the school, but there is none for the pupil.

Social Education

The best-known example of groupwork which aims to affect pupils' behaviour is social education. Because it reaches all pupils, and not just those who behave badly, it obviously has a different focus, but it is similar in that it seeks to affect individual behaviour by using group methods. There is also, I believe, similar confusion in the methods chosen to achieve the stated aims. Social education planners list 'decision-making by pupils' as a priority but then create programmes whose content and delivery encourage acceptance of a prescribed moral code. Much emphasis is placed on teaching pupils skills for decision-making, and I readily acknowledge the need for skills in reaching conclusions. There is, however, a fundamental difference between a programme which helps pupils to decide freely from a range of possibilities, and one which teaches pupils to select a pre-determined right answer. The popularity of programmes like Skills for Adolescents clearly shows the preference of teachers for a didactic approach to behaviour. I seriously doubt the value of such processes but my objections are directed, as they are in one-to-one work, at the dishonesty of any programme which says one thing and does the opposite.

In all groupwork the main issues are power and purpose, which need to be in harmony if a programme is to achieve its objectives. If the purpose is to make pupils behave in a particular way then it follows that the leaders should adopt authoritarian methods of persuasion and coercion. If, on the other hand, the purpose is to give youngsters the right to make decisions, then the leaders' function is to create the atmosphere and structure which will allow clear thinking and rational investigation. As with individuals, a group needs time to move from dependence to independence, but once power has shifted from leaders to members it cannot be taken back even when things go wrong. It is therefore vital that teachers who adopt a democratic methodology are clear about the implications and possible consequences. Many pupils experience a confusing mixture of freedom and tyranny which may be part of growing up, but is likely to cause resentment, cynicism and immature behaviour.

Conclusion

My purpose in this chapter was to ask for clarity and honesty in guidance work. In reaching for that position, we need to acknowledge that guidance teachers are mostly benevolent authoritarians. If they are also honest authoritarians then they will have my respect. However I believe we have a responsibility to prepare young people for the inevitable responsibilities of adulthood, and that means taking the risks and enduring the pain of giving up our power. The difficulties of such a process are undeniable and unavoidable; the rewards to teacher little more than a professional satisfaction at having faced the real issue of education.

Reference

Tacade (1986). *Skills for Adolescence.* Quest International.

Chapter 4

Developing a School Support Service for Children with Social Emotional and Behavioural Difficulties

Alan McLean and Joe Brown

Summary
The paper outlines the rationale for and development of teaching support services for children with social, emotional and behavioural difficulties within mainstream schools in Strathclyde Region. It discusses the problems met during the introduction of the service and the attempts to resolve them. It outlines the potential benefits of a switch from the traditional behaviour change focus to a learning skills model.

1. Rationale

Although there is no empirical evidence to confirm the commonly held assumption that disruption and truancy has greatly increased in recent times, there has certainly been an increasing awareness within education authorities of the need for positive attempts to resolve the problems of disruption and truancy. The one issue from the Committee of Enquiry into Truancy and Indiscipline (SED 1977), usually referred to as the Pack report, to catch the headlines was the recommendation to set up day units for disruptive children. This was then regarded as the most appropriate response to both the problems of the minority of children presenting difficulties and the majority whose educational progress was being disrupted.

In retrospect such segregated provision can be seen as a hastily conceived response to the problem (Tattum 1986), with insufficient thought given to its aims and objectives. Several years on from Pack, The Report of the Committee of Enquiry into Discipline in Schools in England and Wales known as the Elton Report (DES 1989) concluded that 'the balance of advantage lies with the development of support teams'. The HMI report 'Choosing with Care' (SOED 1990) stated that 'the aim must be to prevent the need for alternative education rather than anticipate it'. What has led to this reappraisal of the role of units.

Segregated Provision
The main advantage of segregated schools or units is that the smaller number of pupils can be given more individual attention from teachers within a supportive, structured and caring ethos. However it is now widely acknowledged that the problems of some children may be exacerbated by placement in segregated units. For example social development may be impaired within the sheltered environment;

access to a broad curriculum will certainly be curtailed. The HMI report (op cit) noted 'the curriculum particularly at the secondary stage to be perceived by unit staff as essentially subordinate to pupils' care issues'. Some children respond particularly badly to poor models of behaviour and placement in a unit populated in the majority by children with acting out behaviour problems can lead to a deterioration in their behaviour. Other children with acting out problems have their worst excesses inhibited by the normal expectations and social controls of the teaching staff and peer group within mainstream schooling; once these controls are removed the problems can sometimes spiral out of control. A small number of children find the small group setting too demanding and prefer the anonymity of the larger classroom to the 'hot house' intensity of the unit.

Most of the children involved have low self esteem and placement in alternative provision may be experienced as further rejection and confirmation of their lack of worth and the futility of their efforts. Consequently unit staff have a major task to remotivate them, reassure them of their ability to achieve and renegotiate the relevance of education to them. A further danger is isolation from the peer group in the child's local community. Another common side effect which unit staff have to work hard to counter is the children's feelings of being scapegoated for the problems of the school or family. The pupils placed in units often believe that they have been treated badly by ordinary schools and they feel rejected and resentful.

The pupils considered for placement in segregated provision do not form a readily identifiable normative category of children. The relativity of the assessment process is inevitable as behaviour forms a continuum which cannot be readily compartmentalised into distinct groups (Reynolds, 1989). The cut-off points are arbitrary and the process is plagued with subjectivity (Tattum, 1989). Factors such as the availability of provision are also involved in the process (Booth and Coulby 1987, Smith 1987, and Lloyd-Smith 1984). A further complicating factor is the parallel provision across different agencies - a variation reflecting their differing symptom emphases. In reality most problem childrens' difficulties range across the social, emotional and educational spectrum and most could be placed in any of the provision. Destinations however are determined mainly by the random factor of which agency identifies the problem first.

Reintegration rates are low with most secondary aged pupils remaining in the units until the end of compulsory schooling (Topping, 1983). In part, this is caused by the artificiality of these environments and the curricula followed (Tattum, 1986, Priestley, 1987). Unit staff have viewed the management of difficult behaviour as a greater priority for staff development over the management of the curriculum and this further widens the gap between the unit and mainstream curriculum. The curricular disadvantages will become more marked with the introduction of the 5 to 14 Development Programme when the increasingly structured and sequential curriculum will make it more difficult for children to return to mainstream school. A further difficulty for the units has been to persuade the sending schools to maintain an interest in and link with the pupil. The HMI report considered the communication with mainstream schools from which pupils were received to be generally weak. Criteria determining when a child is ready to return to mainstream school have proved difficult to formulate.

Traditional Assumptions about Behaviour

The assumptions upon which the segregated model was based have been increasingly challenged in recent years. For example emotional and behavioural difficulties were once assumed to be inevitably of long term duration. An early assumption was that when a child's behaviour problems had been 'treated' and 'cured', the new behaviour would generalise and the child would be able to fit back into the mainstream school. There has been little evidence to suggest however that improvements in a child's behaviour established in one context transfers to another.

A further assumption was that the developing skills and expertise of unit staff in managing difficult children would be passed into the mainstream school system. The dissemination of these undoubted skills has not happened to any great extent for a number of reasons. The small number of units are isolated from the mainstream system and no structures have been established to encourage such a dissemination. Unit staff do not always enjoy the necessary level of status and do not share a common language with their mainstream colleagues. The skills are situation specific and not easy to articulate and therefore not readily transferable to ordinary schools.

The main causes of childrens' difficulties have traditionally been thought to relate almost exclusively to child or family factors and the school itself was not regarded as having any significant influence over or responsibility for the child's behaviour. Teachers were therefore able to pass the responsibility for resolving the problems to staff in the segregated facilities and thus discouraged to make any efforts to develop alternative methods of dealing with these children (Booth and Coulby 1987). Research in the last twenty years however has indicated that schools and teachers themselves may have a major influence upon childrens' behaviour. (Kounin 1970, Reynolds 1976, Rutter 1979, Galloway 1985, Mortimore 1988).

Removing difficult pupils from school may be able to help others to make progress but the relationship between the availability of unit places and standards of behaviour in schools is obscure. The evidence suggests however that this has not been accompanied by any noticeable improvement in standards of behaviour. A study of exclusions from schools in Sheffield found that setting up units had no significant effect on the exclusion rates of the schools at which they were established (Galloway 1982). Another study in Strathclyde (McLean 1987) found that processes within the schools appeared to be important in determining whether behaviour would result in exclusion and special placement. McLean concluded that the effectiveness of low excluding schools lay in their preventive approaches to disruption which was rooted in their ideology rather than any radical features of their support systems such as on site units.

To be most effective and to minimise some of the problems outlined above segregated provision needs a clear rationale, a set of criteria for referral, accurate assessment of the needs of each pupil, a programme devised to meet these needs, and clear targets for the early reintegration of each pupil into mainstream classes - features which have to date proved somewhat elusive. The problematic nature of placement in segregated provision is particularly acute for girls. The schools are invariably populated in the main by acting out boys and there is consequently a reluctance to place any girl with interpersonal relationship problems in such a peer group.

The Resource Continuum

Despite the inherent problems in the segregated model, these schools and units continue to provide an essential educational resource to meet the complex needs of a small minority of pupils. Special units manage to work successfully with some of the pupils who are sent to them against all the odds but it requires great skills, effort and perseverance on the part of the staff. It is important for any education authority to achieve a balance between the disadvantages of off-site provision and the real need to maintain a minimum number of places for the most vulnerable group of children. The aim should be to provide a coherent range of integrated support services to meet the full continuum of need. It has never been the intention for the support service to replace segregated provision. Rather the aim has been to remove the need for any further expansion in unit provision and improve the quality of school life for the target group and so prevent later alienation from school. The demand for placement in the units has in fact remained stable and indeed a small number of children on support have been eventually placed in the units.

Most behaviour problems however are now assumed to be learned, transient, and situation specific; they are seen as excesses or deficits of behaviours that are common to all children (Cheeseman and Watts 1985). The school is therefore regarded as the most appropriate agent and locus for preventing, managing or resolving school related behaviour problems.

2. Developments in Behaviour Support

Aims

The service has aimed to offer a proactive and co-ordinated provision of support to children presenting significant school related social, emotional or behavioural problems. The primary service focuses predominantly but not exclusively on the early stages of the primary school. In secondary the main priorities are pupils in the first and second years as well as establishing links with children in the final year of primary. The main aim is to prevent early school based difficulties becoming so entrenched that they require placement outwith school through providing either behaviour change intervention or personal support. The main target group are those children whose access to the curriculum is being severely hindered by their social, emotional or behavioural problems and these problems are predictive of long term adjustment difficulties (Rutter 1990). An additional aim is to develop a wider support role involving group work, whole class strategies and staff consultancy.

The Initial Assessment

Support begins with a short term period of assessment by the support teacher. The information from the assessment is presented at a meeting between school staff, support teacher and the school psychologist. If support is not considered appropriate the class teacher will be provided with advice on what she can do herself. There needs to be a clear commitment and expectation by both school and support service as to who does what and over what time scale. An initial review meeting is held after a maximum of six weeks. Reviews are thereafter held on a regular basis as appropriate when these objectives are reviewed and decisions are made whether any changes are required. Initial involvement entails whenever possible a regular input in short time units of one to one and a half hours. Final withdrawal of support comes after a gradual reduction of support. Only in exceptional circumstances should support continue after the agreed period; all concerned should see themselves as working towards meeting the specified targets by then.

The information gathered during the assessment focuses on the following issues:

1 *The presenting problem*
   What specific problems are concerning the school?
   Which is the priority?
   Where do these difficulties arise?
   When?

How often?
Is there a pattern? (worst after interval, end of morning?)
What effect is the child's difficulties having on the rest of the class?
How does the class respond to the child's difficulties?
Are there other children who present similar difficulties?

2   *The child*
    In which classroom activities does the child best respond?
    Does the child have any learning difficulties?
    What positive attributes does the child have?

3   *Strategies*
    How has the school tried to manage the difficulties so far?
    How has the child responded?
    What additional support does the school require?
    What other supports are available and how can they be integrated into the support plan?

4   *Parents*
    What are the parents' views of the child's needs?
    What has their involvement been in helping resolve the difficulties?
    What is their attitude to a support teacher being involved?

Prior to the assessment meeting the support teacher will meet with the parents to discuss the child's behaviour, their views on support, and to ascertain the extent to which they are likely to co-operate in a programme of intervention.

Predictors of a Positive Response to Support

The factors outlined below have been found to predict a positive response to support -

The problems are
>   identified and tackled early
>   predominantly school based

The family are
>   supportive of the school
>   stable and well in control of child.

The child
>   acknowledges the problem
>   has some insight into the problem
>   is motivated to change

is responsive to support
is interested in some aspects of school
is succeeding in some aspect of school
has good outwith school supports

The school
welcomes and values the support
retains responsibility for the problem
has realistic expectations

Models of Support
A range of practices have developed including the following:
1. In class support: team teaching with either the support or class teacher targeting the referred child.
2. Small group work: involving the target child plus others.
3. Mixture of 1 and 2
4. Extraction - always brief, short term and with clear aims. To effect change the support has to be provided where the problem arises. Most of the gains from working with individual children outwith the classroom unfortunately do not generalise or transfer back to the classroom.
5. Consultancy - to class teachers on issues regarding managing difficult behaviour.
6. Whole Class Approach - A whole class focus sometimes evolves naturally from work with an individual child as a wider perspective is taken in discussions between the support and class teacher. It is important to avoid personalising the problem or blaming the current class teacher and it usually helps to take a historical perspective. It is also a good idea to achieve a staff consensus that this is the top priority class for targeting in such a way. It may also be helpful to plan ahead for the following session. A wide range of rewards strategies have been developed which have proved effective in a group or whole class approach. (McLean 1990)

Role of the Support Teacher
The main role of the support teacher is to directly assist the class teacher by identifying appropriate management strategies, developing individual behaviour and work programmes and resource materials for the targeted child or group. Meetings with the parent on a regular basis is an important aspect of the role particularly with parents who have found difficulty in the past in coming to the

school. Liaison with other agencies is maintained through attendance at assessment and review meetings. Support teachers have experimented with an developed a wide range of alternative support strategies, including play, art, musical and out of school activities, pupil counselling and social groupwork.

What Support can offer

For children support can offer time, attention, someone to listen and provide acceptance and understanding. The support teacher will try to build a positive relationship with the child and adopt an encouraging approach to the child's problems. Better links between school and home will be established. The referred child can expect extra help with his school work as well as his social skills. In these ways the support aims to boost the child's self esteem, confidence and access to the curriculum.

For class teachers support can raise moral and reduce stress by providing encouragement, understanding, reassurance, an acknowledgement and sharing of the problem, a sounding board or safety valve. It offers practical help with class duties, supervision and the curriculum. Constructive discussion with the support teacher can offer an objective assessment of the problem and ideas for behaviour change. Support can provide relief from the pupil or increased opportunities for pupil contact. Support aims to improve communication between the class teacher and the head, the parents, and the psychologist.

3. Initial Problems

Assessment

The support service has had similar problems to those of segregated provision in assessing the presenting problem and the needs of each pupil. The most common attempt to reach an objective assessment has been to use behaviour checklists. There are problems with this approach however. They are little better than discipline records and demoralise the observer; they focus only on the surface behaviours and do not take into account any underlying causal factors. They concentrate on the child's behavioural and personality deficits and fail to look at the child's interaction with the classroom context. The lack of any useful assessment framework has led at times to somewhat vague and general goals being set for support intervention - for example 'to help socialise the child'. In turn this leads to difficulty measuring success and consequent problems deciding when to withdraw support.

Even when a pupil has improved with support, it is often difficult to extricate the support teacher from the school. A common response from the school has been to express their anxiety that the pupil's behaviour will deteriorate if support is withdrawn. One solution to this problem is for a standard time limit to be set on the involvement of support which can be reviewed rather than setting up an open ended contract. The criteria for withdrawal which has evolved is: the child has progressed and achieved the set targets; there is a greater priority elsewhere; no progress has been made after the time limit and there appears little prospect of progress; the school is not backing up the support.

Stress in the Support Role

For most support teachers the role is very different from their previous experience in the classroom and requires a substantial readjustment on their part. The peripatetic nature of the work has the inherent stresses of isolation and not belonging to any of the schools the support teacher visits. A further major stress factor is having to deal with a dual line management of both the school and support service management. It has been helpful to distinguish between strategic accountability to the support service management and operational accountability to the head teacher. A common problem for support teachers is the pressure of unrealistic or inappropriate expectations, for example of being either a miracle worker with an instant cure or a tough disciplinarian. Given the wide range of potential causes underlying childrens' difficulties including home background, emotional or personality problems the number of possible solutions are endless. This can lead to the remit of the support teacher becoming potentially stressful in trying to fulfil the role of counsellor, teacher, psychologist and social worker. This problem can be minimised if the support teacher works as part of a multi disciplinary team. A regular team meeting which offers training, develops mutual support, creates a team spirit and shares good practice is essential.

Deskilling and Learned Helplessness

The existence of any support service can have the unintended side effect of deskilling teachers and reducing their tolerance of the difficulties targeted by the service. If there is an expectation that support will be available for children with behavioural difficulties, a primary school or secondary department with what they consider to be such a child may have a feeling of resentment if support is not forthcoming. Schools can become less willing to reintegrate children from alternative placements without a guarantee of additional support. The introduction of a support service will create a climate which for the first time legitimises schools, particularly primary schools, to be open about their difficulties in managing the behaviour problems of even very young children. Previously it was not professionally acceptable to admit to such problems as it implied incompetence. Consequently the demand for support will quickly expend. A well thought out set of criteria are then required to allow an equitable distribution of the limited resource.

If the class teacher is not kept fully responsible for the child and his difficulties a state of 'learned helplessness' or overdependency on the support teacher can develop leading to a reluctance to give up the support. In the absence of a clear understanding of the role the support teacher can find herself taking on more and more responsibility for the organisation of the class.

Stigma and Labeling

Some children become increasingly entrenched in their problematic pattern of responding. Providing support may inadvertently reinforce their self image as disruptive children who need a teacher to themselves. Some enjoy the notoriety; others are embarrassed, others become annoyed by the presence of the support teacher and can refuse to co-operate. It is important that any such refusal to co-operate with the support teacher is seen for what it is and not necessarily further evidence of emotional disturbance.

Resistance from Class Teachers

i)   *Limited knowledge of the support role*

Much of the initial resistance from class teachers was due to a lack of knowledge about the role of the support teacher. Uncertainty is inevitable over such an innovative and challenging role while in its infancy. Most commonly the class teacher assumes that the support teacher will extract the problem pupil for extensive periods of time. Therefore the first reaction is usually one of relief in anticipation of the problem being taken away albeit temporarily. This expectation can lead to disappointment when the child is not extracted. Other teachers have been negative about the support because of their frustration that the child was not removed from the school, and support makes that event even less likely. Others including guidance staff in secondary schools may be defensive because the provision of support is perceived as an implicit criticism of them.

ii)   *Misbehaving children being given special attention*

Some teachers object to the view that the badly behaved children being given special attention while the majority of children's good behaviour is taken for granted. This feeling can be particularly strong when special rewards are given to referred children for ordinary behaviour. There is concern that the other children will rebel to access these rewards. These anxieties are understandable and have to be talked through. Fortunately most children are exceptionally tolerant and accommodating of what they construe to be especially needy or 'odd' children. The contagion effect is rare because most children do not want is to be seen as 'special'. The majority of childrens' good behaviour is well established and will not deteriorate to access special rewards.

It can be advantageous to make the home the source of any rewards for improved behaviour. This involves the parents in the support plan in a positive way as well as avoiding the difficulties outlined above. Similarly psychologists and social workers may be the source of rewards which signals to the child that his behaviour is a concern not only to the school. Teachers have to be persuaded that the alternative approaches of the support service to problem children are valid, appropriate, well thought out and based on a theoretical rationale. Thus for example they have to accept that these children require extrinsic rewards until they can access the intrinsic rewards open to the other pupils.

iii) *Suspicions from class teachers*

The work of the support teacher can be a potential minefield of suspicions from class teachers. The need for sensitivity is acute where the problem of the referred child is clearly a function of the class teacher's own difficulties in the management of a lively class. The support teacher cannot betray the class teacher and discuss this problem without her knowledge. One approach is for the support teacher to offer advice to the class teacher on general classroom management issues. Another is for the support teacher to negotiate with the class teacher to take the lead and model effective management of the class. This problem must always be regarded as the responsibility of the head teacher and not the support teacher. The work of the support service has highlighted the need for an effective consultancy service for head teachers in managing behaviour problems.

iv) *Antagonism towards the support curriculum*

The vital role of play and games in childrens' development is well documented. Play has in addition a therapeutic role for children in distress many of whom have missed out on the normal play experiences of childhood. The support service has an opportunity to disseminate this supportive aspects of play to schools. Like its secondary equivalent, social groupwork, play should, when used in a structured and planned way, be seen as an essential part of the curriculum for children under stress. Some teachers perceive this as pampering to their needs or rewarding bad behaviour or giving an easy time to the support teacher. Play and group work should be seen as a valid part of any support plan based on an assessment of the child's level of development and readiness for the curriculum. Turn taking, sharing, learning to lose, handling competition, making decisions, developing self expression and temper control are only a few of the skills which have been enhanced through play and social groupwork. Play helps develop a child's readiness for the verbal passive and abstract aspects of the more formal curriculum. If for example the child still needs a high level of activity with concrete materials it is futile to insist that he concentrates for long periods of time on formal written work.

Chapter 4

4. Guidelines for Effective Support

Many of these problems have been resolved by the development and implementation of the following guidelines.

Primary Schools

Ownership of or responsibility for the problem is a key issue which needs to be addressed at the outset. The class and head teacher should retain overall responsibility for the pupils.

The aims of support must be communicated to staff to set realistic expectations.

A support plan must be devised and agreed upon between the psychologist, class teacher, head teacher and support teacher.

Support plans should involve specific and clear aims involving targets which can be evaluated.

Support should be seen as an enhancement, and not a substitute for other support systems.

The parents should be in full agreement with and willing to co-operate with the support plan.

Time should be allocated for the class teacher to consult with support staff.

The school should be willing to experiment with alternative support strategies and be prepared to consider rewarding targeted behaviour.

Support should be subject to regular reviews to collate all available information, evaluated whether the aims are being achieved and plan any future support.

The class teacher and parent should attend all assessment and review meetings.

Secondary School

All of the above plus -

1. *(Support as a) whole-school policy*
   a. The senor management team should be seen to be committed to and actively involved in the development of the school support programme.
   b. Specific aims for the support programme must be agreed between the senior staff of the school, support staff and the divisional steering group.
   c. It would be helpful if other staff can be encouraged to become involved in individual support programmes.

Chapter 4

2. *Overview*
   a. An overview of all support and discipline systems in the school should be maintained by senior members of staff.
   b. The aims of the support programme should be compatible with the school's policies for discipline, guidance and learning support.
   c. Support programmes should operate in tandem with, not sequential to, the discipline system.

3. *Consultation*
   a. Support staff should be consulted wherever possible when a referred pupil is being considered for exclusion.
   b. Support staff should always contribute to reports to outside agencies.
   c. Support staff should be allowed to attend relevant review meetings of referred pupils in and out of school.

4. *Referrals*
   a. Clear procedures and explicit referral criteria should be agreed.
   b. It should be accepted that the preventative nature of support implies earlier rather than later referral.

Despite these guidelines however, some problems have persisted in the delivery of the support service. Some of these problems relate to how the presenting difficulties have been construed by schools and the service. The final section of this paper discusses a model which has recently emerged from practice which views childrens' behaviour problems from a 'learning skills' perspective rather than the traditional behaviour deficit model. The emphasis is now on skills which need to be learned as opposed to behaviour which needs to be eliminated.

5. Reframing the Problem

Behaviour problems have been an issue which the educational establishment has traditionally tended to overlook. There have, for example, been until recently few instances of professional development courses or specialist training courses in managing behaviour problems; the issue is rarely discussed in pre-service training courses. Children with behaviour problems appear to even more marginalised than children with learning difficulties and special needs. There is a prevalent view that children with behavioural difficulties should not be maintained in ordinary school if they inhibit the educational progress of others. This is unfair discrimination as they are not the only group likely to inhibit others' learning but the only group about which this view is taken. As these children come in disproportionate numbers from deprived areas, the most vulnerable group are further discriminated against.

Just as the Warnock Report argued against the categorisation of special needs, there are strong arguments against a separate category of emotional and behavioural difficulty. It would be unfortunate if the developments in behaviour support further reinforces this separate model. Providing a specialist sector of support must not confirm the common notion that behaviour is distinct from learning, detached from the curriculum, and beyond the teacher's influence or responsibility. It is unfortunate that this group of children are dealt with in separate regional and national policy documents which appear to enjoy a less positive reception than policies concerning special needs or learning difficulties. It is important therefore that any specialist sectors are seen as closely integrated into a general support service sharing the same model of understanding and responding to childrens' learning problems be they based upon their emotional, learning, sensory or physical difficulties. Consequently behaviour support may be more appropriately considered a specialist arm of peripatetic learning support in the primary sector and of learning support departments in the secondary sector. Only in this way will the vital importance of the curriculum be seen to apply to all children with school related problems.

This model argues strongly for an emphasis on co-operative teaching and staff development rather than pupil extraction. It is significant that most regional policies on learning difficulties taking their lead from the HMI Progress Report on Learning Difficulties (SED 1978) argues strongly for these roles for learning support staff. The same arguments apply equally forcibly when considering children with behaviour problems. Reward charts, home links, group work and individual counselling are useful adjuncts but are of limited value as the main focus of the work.

Towards a 'Learning Skills' Model

This perceptual shift would be facilitated if the presenting problems were reframed from issues about changing misbehaviour to developing the classroom interaction skills which are important precursors of learning. Apart from a small minority of withdrawn children, most children referred to the support service have either attention seeking or ill tempered interaction styles. A study of the cases referred to the support service revealed for example that one of the key classroom skills which all of the children had poorly developed, was coping with negative feedback, particularly teacher reprimands and punishments. A checklist of such classroom interaction skills has been devised and is being currently piloted by the support service. (See Appendix) This checklist provides a useful structure for the assessment and planning meeting between the class teacher, support teacher and psychologist.

Advantages of the Learning Skills Model

i)   *More Relevant Focus*

A focus on behaviour alone which assumes an ability to behave is relevant within a disciplinary perspective but its utility in a supportive approach is questionable. The skills model deals with misbehaviour as surface phenomenon and concentrates on those underlying causes which can be addressed in the classroom. It focuses on childrens' classroom interaction skills which are essentially appropriate behaviours for the classroom. It examines the child's interaction with the curriculum, the teacher and the peer group. The skills model is proactive and focuses on the antecedents of misbehaviour rather than the consequences. This approach allows a diagnostic analysis within a curricular framework which monitors change over time as opposed to a fixed assessment of the child's behavioural and personality deficits.

ii)   *More Useful Information*

The trouble with most assessments with the traditional emphasis on misbehaviour is that they provide a great deal of redundant information which offers little additional insight into the problem and proves irrelevant in the search for effective strategies. This model encourages a more positive and balanced perspective of the child's strengths and weaknesses. The information collated is not only more useful but also more reliable because it is less contaminated by the teacher's attitude. The behaviour approach tries and fails to objectify what is essentially subjective.

iii)   *A More Positive Outcome*

Rather than the often disheartening effect of the misbehaviour model this approach has more potential to change teachers' perceptions and enhance their insight into problem children. It discourages the defensive and frustrating punitive approaches and instead leads to a positive development plan involving specific teaching objectives. Rather than having to try to stop unwanted behaviour, the aim is to develop skills which the child has not yet acquired - an aim with which teachers are more comfortable and for which they have been trained. It helps give a starting point by identifying the priority discrete and achievable skills to be targeted in reward programmes. Related curricular materials are becoming increasingly available (Tacade 1986, 1991, Alwyn and Freed 1988, Borba 1989,

Bond 1986, Leach and Wooster 1986, Waters 1991). Evaluation of Tacade's 'Skills for Adolescence Programme' revealed that young people who had completed the course were able to communicate more effectively with peers and adults, played truant less often and had fewer discipline problems. (Parsons, 1988.)

Additional Advantages

The 'learning skills' model has additional advantages over the 'behaviour change' model. It offers a conceptual framework which is readily understood by classroom teachers, parents and children. It gives both the class and support teacher a clear focused agenda and helps avoid problems associated with the open ended nature of the support role and should also help overcome initial teacher uncertainty and resistance. Both behaviour and skills in reality form a continuum, but skills are more easily construed in this way than behaviour which tends to be seen in black and white terms. The skills model is also more open to a 'needs' rather than 'deeds' perspective.

The 'misbehaviour' approach has often resulted in a high level of parental resistance probably due to parents feelings of being blamed for their child's behaviour. Similarly pupil non-co-operation is a common result of feeling picked on for being 'bad'. The 'skills' approach is less threatening and humiliating to children and parents alike and consequently more likely to enlist parental and pupil co-operation. It is also more open to self assessment and therefore more useful as both an indicator of the child's level of insight and as a counselling device leading to greater insight in the child. The skills approach retains the responsibility for behaviour with the class teacher and also taps into the expertise of learning support staff. It is closely related to the objectives of social group workers from the Social Work Department and could provide a useful common focus for joint work. Finally the skills model has universal application and value for all children not just the badly behaved group.

Implications of the 5 - 14 Development Programme

The 5 - 14 programme provides both potential difficulties and opportunities for this group of children. The risk from the 5 - 14 programme comes from the increasing importance given to group work and co-operative learning where classroom interaction skills are essential. This approach will place more and more demands upon children with particular difficulties in this skill area and could inadvertently lead to an increase in perceived behavioural problems.

There are however opportunities to improve the responsiveness of the education system to the needs of this group of children. The key aim of the programme is appropriate differentiation to offer all pupils a curriculum which is both appropriate and challenging. Although there has been recent progress in teachers' ability and willingness to differentiate their curriculum and methodology according to childrens' learning capabilities, we now need to facilitate differential expectations and treatment of children in terms of their classroom interaction styles and readiness for independent and co-operative learning. Teachers may sometimes confuse uniformity of response with the notion of fairness and feel they cannot treat pupils differently because the children will resent the differential treatment. This however is perhaps an adult perception which teachers project onto children.

There have not until now been relevant sets of attainment targets available for personal and social skills. A start to this area has been made in RDG 5 Personal and Social Development although the concepts developed to date are somewhat abstract, lack operations clarity and will consequently be difficult to assess. The 5 - 14 programme's clearly stated sequences of objectives and continuous assessment will however facilitate individual programming and encourage the sort of analytical thinking outlined above about component skills which lends itself to more detailed sequences of learning objectives in particular areas (Maxwell 1991) - for example classroom interaction skills.

Conclusions

The obvious advantage of the support service over segregated provision is the retention of referred children in school and the avoidance of the potential hazards of segregated placement. The problems are tackled where they occur in the classroom; the contribution of the school in both the creation and management of the problems is acknowledged and alternative practical strategies are developed in partnership with class teachers. The approach is proactive and flexible with the support teacher's role negotiable. Good practice can be developed and more readily disseminated through the mainstream system. The provision can cover a larger number of children than could be catered for in specialist units and any beneficial effects extend beyond the targeted child. The key issue in determining the effectiveness of support is whether ownership of the problems is retained by the school to enable the support service to work in partnership with the family and school to help resolve the problems.

Many of the initial problems have been resolved with the implementation of the guidelines to school. The move from the 'Behaviour Change' model to the 'Learning Skills' model shows great potential for a further increase in effectiveness. The key tasks are to identify the unlearned interaction skills which the child's misbehaviour represents and to devise strategies to teach these skills. This model provides a sharper focus and structure which is compatible with other support services and offers an accurate assessment of the needs of each pupil and clear targets for any intervention.

Chapter 4

Appendix: Assessing Children's Classroom Interaction Style

1. Response to the Curriculum

A **(Readiness for) Independent Learning**
Being on time
Listening
Paying attention
Following instructions
Getting started
Getting self organised
Coping with routines
Looking after belongings
Responding to new experiences/challenges
Staying on task
Using resources and equipment
Asking for help appropriately
Persevering despite difficulty
Staying in seat
Sitting still
Keeping to acceptable noise level
Coping with distractions
Completing tasks of which capable
Showing pride in achievements
Moving to next task

B **(Readiness for) Co-operative Learning**
Taking part in discussion
Taking turns
Sharing materials and equipment
Allowing others to work
Working cooperatively
Coping with teasing
Handling competition
Dealing sensitively with others' feelings

2. Response to Adults
Accepting directions/instructions
Sharing adult attention

Meeting Special Educational Needs:
A Scottish Perspective

Complying with rules - accepting limits
Accepting punishments
Recognising authority
Responding to praise and other rewards
Speaking to adults in appropriate manner
Coping with criticism from adults
Responding to reprimands
Responding to adult help
Getting adults' approval
Tuning in to teacher's mood
Accepting just consequences
Controlling temper
Tolerating frustration

Notes

Ratings can be completed for different contexts - for example the classroom (with and without support), unstructured situations in school, at home and attending an intermediate treatment group.

For teacher assessment use a 1 to 4 rating scale -

0 - no evidence of skills
1 - below average skill level for the class
2 - average skill level
3 - above average skill level

For self assessment use a 10 point rating scale

References

Alwyn, T and Freed, M (1988). *Transactional Analysis for Kids.* Addison Wesley.

Apter, S J (1982). *Troubled Children, Troubled Systems.* Pergamon Press, Oxford.

Bond, T (1986). *Games for Social and Life Skills.* Nichols, London.

Borba, M (1989). *Self Esteem Builders.* Jalmar Press, California.

Cheeseman, P L and Watts, P E (1985). *Positive Behaviour Management - a Manual for Teachers.* Croom Helm.

DES (1989). *Discipline in Schools.* Report of the Committee of Enquiry Department of Education and Science and the Welsh Office, HMSO.

HMI (1990). *Choosing With Care - Provision for pupils with Behavioural, Social and Emotional Difficulties.* Scottish Education Department, HMSO.

Jones, N (ed) (1989). *School Management and Pupil Behaviour: Education and Alienation Series.* The Falmer Press, Lowes.

Jones, N and Southgate, T (ed) (1989). *The Management of Special Needs in Ordinary Schools.* Routeledge, London.

Kounin (1970). *Discipline and Group Management in Classrooms.* Holt Reinhart and Winston.

Leech, N and Wooster, A (1986). *Personal and Social Skills - a Practical Approach for the Classroom.* Religious and Moral Education Press, London.

Lloyd-Smith, M (ed) (1984). *Disruptive Schooling: The Growth of the Special Unit.* John Murray Ltd., London.

Maxwell, W (1991). The 5 - 14 Development Programme - implications for the Psychological Services. *Scottish Division of Educational and Child Psychology Newsletter* 2, pp 29-38.

Mortimore, P (1988). *School Matters - The Junior Years.* Open Books.

McLean, A (1987). After the belt: school processes in low exclusion schools. *School Organization* 7 (3), pp 303-310.

McLean, A (1990). *Promoting Positive Behaviour in the Primary School.* Strathclyde Regional Council.

Parsons, C (1988). *An Evaluation of Skills for Adolescence on behalf of the DES.* Christchurch College, Canterbury.

Rutter, M, et al (1979). *Fifteen Thousand Hours: Secondary Schools and their Effects on Pupils.* Open Books. Wells, Somerset.

Rutter, M and Robbins, L (1990). *Straight and Devious Pathways from Childhood to Adulthood.* Cambridge University Press.

Scottish Education Department (1978). *The Education of Pupils with Learning Difficulties in Primary and Secondary Schools; a Progress Report by Her Majesty's Inspectorate.* HMSO.

Tacade (1986). *Skills for Adolescence.* Quest International.

Tacade (1991). *Skills for the Primary School Child.* Quest International.

Tattum, D (1982). *Disruptive Pupils in Schools and Units.* John Wiley and Sons, Chichester.

Tattum, D P (1989). Alternative approaches to disruptive behaviours. In Jones (1989).

Tattum, D (ed) (1986). *The Management of Disruptive Pupil Behaviour in Schools.* John Wiley and Sons.

Topping, K J (1983). *Educational Systems for Disruptive Adolescents.* Croom Helm, London.

Waters, F (1991). *Lessons for Living.* Strathclyde Psychological Service.

Chapter 5

Youth Strategies in Scotland
Tim Pickles

Youth strategies have been developed in several local authorities during the past ten years as a collaborative response to the needs and difficulties presented by primarily adolescent young people below the school leaving age. These strategies tend to be a uniquely Scottish approach to the problem. Elsewhere in Britain, such collaborative practices tend to be restricted to particular aspects of work with children in difficulty, such as child abuse or juvenile justice. The broader approach, which has always been a hallmark of Scottish child care, has permitted the development of youth strategies, although as this chapter will show, their emergence has not been without significant difficulties in the translation of fine principles into real practice on the ground.

The Scottish context for work with young people in trouble

There have been regular calls from government departments during the past 15 years exhorting statutory agencies to work more closely together in a variety of fields. More recently, as the political culture has changed, this has been extended to include closer partnership with voluntary and independent sector providers of services. Yet it is only in the last year or two that central government guidance has been issued on how this should be achieved.

There are many inherent problems in the development of corporate working arrangements. Not least amongst these is the understandable desire of many departmental managers to foster and protect their own services at a time when cutbacks have been frequently threatened. Corporate strategies became possible with the creation of chief executive departments during the last reorganisation of local government. The chief executive is the most senior officer of the authority and has a responsibility to coordinate policies across all council services. Many chief executives created senior management teams in which the directors of different departments meet together to integrate their policies and ensure a consistency of approach.

This 'top-level' coordination produced some impressive policies. Senior officers working together, often with elected members in joint member/officer groups, devised such policies as Strathclyde's *Social Strategy for the Eighties* which were designed to influence and inform all other policies throughout the council. However, at a more practical level, the degree of co-operation found amongst senior managers was less easy to replicate in area offices, practice teams and

Chapter 5

schools where senior staff time was often consumed by the daily tasks of managing affairs within the organisation. Liaison procedures were established between local agencies to maintain communication but this was often far from a genuine working collaboration and the sharing of resources. Nevertheless, in different parts of the country throughout the eighties, individuals were striving to overcome these difficulties and produce a more co-ordinated response to the needs of adolescents which would enable professionals from different disciplines to work together for the benefit of the youngster.

Kevin Gill and Tim Pickles, in their book on youth strategies have identified three main factors leading to the creation of youth strategies: the Scottish children's hearing system, the existence of the Intermediate Treatment Resource Centre (ITRC) as an independent national agency advocating for greater collaboration, and the transfer of funding for residential schools from central to local government. (1989)

The legislative framework for responding to young people thought to be at risk and in need of compulsory measures of care was established by the Kilbrandon Committee in 1964. The Children's Hearing system is based on decision-making by a number of independent people who do not have vested interests in any one of the services. Furthermore, these decision-makers are obliged by the legislation to have regard only to the best interests of the young person, and not to the protection or interests of the wider community or institutions within it. The Reporter is an independent officer who receives information from any source about young people who may be in difficulty; it is his decision as to whether any formal action is required. He can speak to any of the agencies involved with the young person and to the family. If formal care measures are likely, he can convene a Hearing at which the young person and his or her family will sit around a table with three lay Panel Members to discuss relevant reports on the young person and decide what course of action should be followed.

The hearings' system is an open one. It seeks consensus where possible and it strives to involve children, parents and concerned agencies in determining appropriate responses. It does not divide groups and allocate blame between them. At its heart is a focus on the needs of the child as the primary consideration. This system therefore tends to avoid confrontation, and creates a more fertile environment for different people to meet together and share responsibility for the needs of young people.

The ITRC was a voluntary agency funded by central government to promote and develop community-based services for young people at risk and in trouble throughout Scotland. It was instrumental in the early 1980's in the creation of new intermediate treatment and groupwork projects for such youngsters, and it worked closely with social work managers, area teams and others in the development of policies in this area. It has always been clear that the difficulties of many young people cannot be neatly parcelled between different departments. Truancy, for example, is a classic example of a problem which is first dealt with by education but often becomes the responsibility of social work. The ITRC worked with several agencies to develop preventive approaches, and to secure the most appropriate response to different problems. It became obvious that closer working partnerships were often needed between teachers, social workers, youth workers and others on the ground if such responses were to have greater effect.

Working with Strathclyde staff, the ITRC produced a policy proposal in 1982 which first coined the phrase 'youth strategy' to describe a strategic approach to such problems including the allocation of lead responsibilities. Three years later, aspects of this thinking found their way into Strathclyde's *Care Strategy* which set out the social work department's policy towards young people. The youth strategy approach was taken up by staff in other regions and gradually found its way into several policy statements. In 1985, the Confederation of Scottish Local Authorities produced a report recommending that all local authorities should develop joint policies for difficult and disturbed adolescents. This move was emphasised again in the *Review of IT in Scotland* commissioned by the Scottish Office and undertaken by the ITRC.

In 1986, central government transfered responsibility and financial resources for residential schools (formerly known as List D schools) to regional authorities. Prior to this, any council which placed a child in a List D residential school did not have to meet all of the costs from its own resources. The transfer of responsibility placed residential schools on a par with residential homes (some with education) run by social work departments. It now made sense to develop a coherent approach to the use of these various resources. It was also possible to reduce the expenditure on residential schools as alternative forms of community-based care were developed. This could only be achieved through an integrated approach and a youth strategy provided a suitable vehicle.

What are youth strategies?

Youth strategies can be considered at two different levels. At the macro-level, a youth strategy provides a framework for the overall co-ordination of resources to young people in trouble ensuring that they benefit from the best range of services. At the micro-level, a youth strategy comprises examples of different professional field workers working together for the benefit of individual youngsters.

The policy level youth strategy sets the context for all work with adolescents presenting difficulties. It will have been agreed invariably between officers of the education and social work departments at least, and may have been extended to include representation and agreement with the Reporter, health officers and the police. The youth strategy is the framework which guides all action. For example, the strategy may establish liaison groups in every school or area team which should consider all cases of children in difficulty before formal measures of suspension or care proceedings are taken. The strategy may require regular monitoring of children coming to the attention of the formal authorities in order to determine what the principal causes of disruption are, so that preventive measures can be devised in response. The strategy may set out minimum criteria which have to be met before any child can be considered for placement outside their normal family, thereby regulating access to residential facilities and encouraging the development of less intrusive community-based intervention and support.

Such youth strategy policies will, in turn, lead to the establishment of field practice examples of youth strategies in action. Most of these will be typified by staff from more than one agency working alongside each other without the customary professional obstacles to sharing resources and joint working. Different professionals might agree to contribute their varying viewpoints to a joint assessment of a young person without the necessity for her removal from home into a residential assessment centre. Social workers, teachers and youth workers might be employed (or seconded) to work together in one centre providing limited education and family support in an effort to re-integrate pupils into conventional schools and family homes. A teacher might be assisted by a social worker or IT worker in the provision of a regular groupwork programme either in or out of ordinary school, to help a group of secondary pupils adjust to the pressures of the school.

Examples of youth strategies in practice

Most of the larger regional councils in Scotland have now adopted youth strategies. This section focuses on a few examples to show the range of criteria and provision contained within the policies.

Lothian Region was the first council to formally develop a joint statement between the education and social work departments in 1983. This document was aimed at coping with some of the region's most difficult youngsters. It set out four explicit principles for staff:

1. Problems associated with children's behaviour or circumstances should be dealt with wherever possible by keeping the child in his/her local community, using the resources of the family and other local resources in a flexible manner.

2. Children who are at risk of having to leave home or who are at risk of being excluded from school or who have a special educational need should be jointly

assessed and in some cases jointly reviewed.

3. Both the education and social work departments will endeavour to contribute day and group work provision as an alternative to the residential care of adolescent children where this is appropriate.

4. No child should be recommended for residential care unless:

    a) he/she has no home (including a substitute home) in the community which can, with appropriate support, provide an adequate degree of control or care, or

    b) he/she is at risk to himself/herself or others in the community, or

    c) he/she has a medical, psychiatric or special educational needs which can only be dealt with in a residential context, and/or it is in the child's best interest which cannot be met in any other way.

This proved to be a far sighted statement although for several years it proved hard to achieve the intended results. Although the commitment was clear, the implementation process was not, and children continued to be moved out of the community in various ways. Eventually, these loopholes were substantially plugged by the addition of a fifth principle:

5. No child of primary school age should be sent outside Lothian Region on a List G school placement without the prior specific approval of the education committee.

This ensured that staff began to consider joint assessments of young people in the community. This process was considerably helped by the gradual establishment in every regional secondary school of a School Liaison Group (SLG). Convened by the school (usually a depute head or principal teacher with guidance responsibilities), the SLG considers individual pupils in difficulty on a regular basis. The meeting is attended by representatives of the school, education welfare service and social work departments. In most cases, the education psychologist, local community education officer and interested voluntary agency representatives will be invited to attend together with the school's medical officer if appropriate. The SLG provides a forum for jointly discussing young people's difficulties. The ideas and perspectives of several agencies are brought to bear. Staff from one organisation can offer expertise and resources to another. The prevention of further difficulties becomes the goal through joint problem solving, rather than the earlier model of responding to a succession of crises. The SLGs are able not only to consider the difficulties of individual pupils, but also to assess the general picture over time and comment on aspects of the school's organisation or functioning which might need attention.

The school liaison groups are not panaceas for the difficulties of adolescents. Many pupils continue to 'slip through the net'. Some pupils have to be suspended quickly for serious disciplinary offences before an SLG meeting can be convened. It is questionable to what extent truanting pupils who are also disruptive when in school are brought to the attention of an SLG; in some cases, it may be easier for the school to 'forget' about some awkward young people as they approach the school leaving date. The majority of referrals to the SLG are also made by the school: there is less reason for them to consider cases of young people who are well behaved in school but are experiencing difficulties either at home or on the street which are concerning the social work department.

Some Lothian pupils do need more intensive support than the resources which are available through teachers and fieldworkers attending the SLG. Lothian is now establishing a network of centres which are able to provide both day and evening care for small numbers of adolescents. Such centres have existed in Edinburgh for several years and are now re-establishing part-time education provision as part of their programme. A new centre in West Lothian is run by a joint team of teachers, social workers and community education workers. Whilst accepting referrals into its day education or evening groupwork programmes, it seeks to run these in partnership with the mainstream services so as not to stigmatise these children further. Thus the day education programme is only ever part-time: all pupils must spend part of each week in their ordinary school. The evening groupwork programme involves area office social workers, many of whom will have clients participating in the group.

The Ferguslie Park area of Paisley in Strathclyde Region comprises a large council housing estate with more than its fair share or social and environmental problems. The local social work team has always been predominantly child care focused because of the large numbers of referrals to the Reporter and the substantial numbers of young people subject to statutory measures of care.

Some years ago, the intermediate treatment and social work teams were concerned about the service they were offering in the provision of reports to the children's hearing for young people referred for the first time. These reports were usually prepared by a social worker after visiting the family and interviewing the young person. Because of the numbers being prepared, the amount of time devoted to each, and the depth of information collected was sometimes minimal. The social workers and IT staff agreed to establish a regular 'pre-panel assessment group' (ie. pre-hearing) which would meet on a weekly basis. With the cooperation of the families, children referred to their first hearing would attend the group for six consecutive weeks. The staff used the group to observe and collect assessment information about the youngster which was then collected and presented in a written report for the Reporter's office. This report would invariably end with a recommendation on whether further statutory care measures were required in which case a hearing would be convened.

As the group became more established it came to be viewed as an ideal and effective way of gathering relevant information easily and effectively. It utilised the expertise of different professionals without making undue demands on scarce resources. In time, other agencies took an interest in the work of the group. Whilst local schools were never formally involved, they were kept informed and consulted about the final recommendations.

The results from the pre-panel assessment group were impressive. Over a four year period, whilst the number of young people taken into the group dropped from 31 to 10, the number of first time referrals placed on statutory supervision to the social work department dropped from 17 to 3 respectively.

Tayside has not developed a formal youth strategy as such but it has recently reorganised many of its child care services under its *Children in Crisis* policy, and many of the changes are designed to foster collaborative working practices. The principal development is the creation of Children's Resource Centres. These seek to bring together under one roof many of the services for young people previously offered by the social work department through different specialisms. Resource centres are being established to serve each of the different divisions on a local basis. The centre managers have access to staff skilled in assessment work, supervision, groupwork, preparation for fostering, community carers, emergency care, short term care and preparation for independence. Thus individual young people can be supported through their changing needs from the resources available within one centre.

It is also intended that resource centre staff will operate in a flexible way covering different duties (within limits) from this range as the pattern of demand changes with time. A key idea in the Tayside proposals is not merely to minimise the use of long-term residential care, but also to recognise that young people may move in and out of different forms of residential and non-residential facilities quite quickly. This can be done in a co-ordinated way if there is a comprehensive care plan for the child. The resource centres are thus concerned with breaking down some of the barriers which have previously existed between different facilities, and ensuring that services can be offered in a more flexible way with adequate planning and monitoring of the changing circumstances.

Moves are under discussion in Tayside to ensure that the education department is also able to contribute to this process. Two large regional conferences have been held under the title 'Joining Forces' in an effort to bring staff from both department together. There are several initiatives in which teachers work alongside social work staff, and the voluntary sector has been instrumental in demonstrating ways in which this can be achieved through Dundee projects run by Barnardo's and NCH.

The difficulties in making youth strategies work

Whilst youth strategies may seem to make excellent sense in the provision of services for disruptive and disturbing children, it is no accident that they have taken so long to become established – and then only on a fragmented basis across Scotland. The difficulties inherent in getting to the point where such collaborative statements can actually be proposed, never mind being implemented in practice, should not be under-estimated.

The process of generating and managing inter-agency policies is fraught with difficulties. Someone has to initiate the process, and whoever this is tends to be perceived as acting out of a vested interest either to pass problems to someone else or to expand their own role at the expense of another. Many joint initiatives have only come about as a result of independent action by less involved individuals. In some authorities, the lead has been taken by the chief executive's department which is not directly involved in the provision of services to children but can require co-ordination amongst others. In Lothian, it was the elected members who created the first joint working groups and asked their officers to follow the practice.

Some innovatory work has been developed by voluntary agencies seeking to demonstrate how joint professional practice can work and indirectly bringing other disciplines together perhaps through a joint advisory or management group. The ITRC acted as an independent advisory body for several authorities working with them to devise collaborative statement and working procedures.

This experience has shown that there are two crucial areas on which agreement has to be reached for any joint practice to succeed – shared objectives and shared values.

Unless all the parties agree to the end goals of the policy, the chances of it succeeding are remote. An obvious example concerns the approach to disruptive school pupils. If the school merely wants to remove a pupil from the school roll, whilst the social work department wants to resist any referral to the Reporter which might result in statutory supervision of the child by themselves, there is little scope for co-operation. To make progress, both parties need to agree, for example, that whilst this youngster is not conforming well at school at present, every effort should be made to find proper education which will enable the child to remain living at home. This objective offers a common base from which all parties can contribute suggestions and resources. At the macro-level, partners to a youth strategy have to agree on the benefits of community-based forms of care and response. One region, for example, decided that neither the education nor the social work department could utilise residential resources without the agreement of the other. In this way, a dialogue was possible which could lead to the transfer of resources from one form of provision to another. This would be less likely to happen if one agency simply had overall control of its own resources as there would be less incentive for critical appraisal.

The absence of shared values makes it particularly difficult for staff from different disciplines or agencies to actually work together. The disruptive pupil in school provides the example again. For the social worker, the concern is the best interest of the child; for the harassed classroom teacher, this concern is likely to be equally matched by the need to teach and protect other pupils in the class who would probably learn far better without the disruptive pupil's presence and influence. At a more fundamental level, different staff approach the work with very different beliefs. Some regard young people as innocent victims of family circumstances; other see children as knowingly aware and responsible for their own actions; yet others regard the social and political culture as major determinants of an individual's behaviour. These value systems are deep-seated and ingrained. Most of us are not used to exploring our personal values with colleagues, especially colleagues about whose professional background we know little. It is little surprise that traditionally there is scepticism and distrust of the work of other professionals outside our own disciplines. For joint working to be truly effective, those involved have to start sharing and exploring these issues together to give themselves a common platform on which to work for the benefit of young people.

This has led to the development of joint training initiatives designed to bring managers and fieldworkers from the same area but different agencies together. Such training tends to begin by examining the myths and prejudices which one group has of another. The stereotypes are looked at for what they are. This can lead to a deeper examination at the actual contributions and restrictions each professional group has to make to work with young people. In the process, people will share values, techniques, frustrations, and ideas for practical change. It is these ideas, worked at together by mixed groups of staff, which can prove a fertile ground for genuine collaboration in practice. The process of such joint training also needs careful handling and negotiation so that no one agency is perceived as telling another what to do. The use of outside trainers can be one way of avoiding this 'ownership' problem until the process of joint working is well established.

Finally the problem of accountability in shared working has to be overcome. Each person involved is accountable to their own agency or department, but it is this retreat to professional disciplines which has made the creation of youth strategies so difficult in the past. These formal lines of accountability need to be recognised but set on one side in the practice. For the benefits of joint working to appear, experience has shown that the ultimate accountability of those involved is to the young person. This is the 'customer' whom the practice is designed to benefit. If the youth strategy staff can also regard themselves as primarily accountable to the child, it is an appropriate way of developing both the policies and the practice whose roots lie in the child-centred approach of the Scottish welfare system.

The future for youth strategies

Youth strategies in Scotland have shown themselves to be an effective approach to the problems presented by disruptive and disturbed adolescents. Whilst not embodying any specific techniques, the processes which encourage joint working and collaborative problem solving have proved effective in meeting child care needs.

The present climate pushes in two contradictory directions at once. The squeeze on local services means that many agencies are less willing to invest time and energy in joint working when there are so many demands for services which, in the short term, it is easier for them to meet alone. As a result, some agencies may look to ways of withdrawing from partnership working arrangements. At the same time, there is political pressure to seek more effective uses for resources, and considerable endorsement of the need for partnership arrangements often involving statutory and voluntary or independent sector providers. In some cases, funding is only available where such partnerships can be shown to exist. Thus joint strategies in one form or another are likely to continue in the future although the motivation for their creation may change.

Joint practices are developing elsewhere in relation to child abuse, care in the community, crime prevention and inner-city rejuvenation. It seems likely that the collaborative strategic approaches pioneered in Scotland will eventually find echoes in other forms of provision and in other parts of the country.

References

Gill, K., and Pickles, T. (1989) *Active Collaboration: Joint Practice and Youth Strategies.* Intermediate Treatment Resource Centre.

ITRC (1986). *Review of IT in Scotland.* Intermediate Treatment Resource Centre.

Jones, N. (1990). *Agency Collaboration and Disaffected Pupils.* Falmer Press.

Chapter 6

Children's Hearings and School Problems

Malcolm Schaffer

Background

Any serious student of the Children's Hearing System needs to start by referring to the Kilbrandon Report 1964. This is not just because it is the source of the entire system, but because it provides an invaluable summary of the previous history of juvenile justice in Scotland and even more importantly, sets out the basic philosophy of the system in words which are as important and relevant today as they were when the Hearing System started.

The theme of the Report was to reject a narrow crime/punishment approach for dealing with children in trouble but instead promote 'the application of an educative principle which cannot hope to operate with any measure of success except under a procedure which from the outset seeks to establish the individual child's needs in the light of the fullest possible information as to his circumstances, personal and environmental'.

The educative principle which is the cornerstone of the Kilbrandon Report was meant in its widest sense - that of social education. In this context, it is worth noting one major recommendation of Kilbrandon which never saw the light of day. This proposed the creation of a new Department of Social Education which would have fallen under the responsibility of the Director of Education. This Department would have taken responsibility for child care, child guidance, education welfare and school attendance. This part of the report, however, was never implemented and the different functions of that proposed Department were split up. Child care, which was to form the main service to Children's Hearings, fell under the control of the Director of Social Work. As we shall see later, the net result of this was to create a distancing between education and the Children's Hearing System which has only recently been narrowed.

Kilbrandon's main focus was upon juvenile delinquency which formed the large percentage of referrals to the Juvenile Courts then in existence. In relation to school attendance it was stated that 'truancy, so persistent and serious as to justify Court proceedings fortunately arises fairly rarely'.

The Report, however, did go on to acknowledge that where it did exist 'persistent truancy is in many cases a manifestation of emotional disturbance, often attributable to factors in the home and family background'.

In such cases Kilbrandon identified the same crucial aspects of investigation and decision making as in cases of juvenile delinquency, namely 'the need for assessment of individual needs, the need to take into account all factors in a child's background which may be contributing to a child being in trouble, the need for early detection and for intervention only where needed and which should be flexible to each child's needs'.

The Kilbrandon Report led to the Social Work (Scotland) Act 1968 which created the machinery for the Children's Hearing System. Its functioning today in relation to problems at school is what the remainder of this chapter will be devoted to exploring.

The Reporter

One of the leading books on the Children's Hearing System compared the Reporter with the Roman God Janus (Bruce & Spencer 1976). Regrettably, it was not meant as a comment on the divine quality of the Reporter's decision making! Rather it provided a suitable metaphor of the functions of the Reporter - standing on the threshold of the Hearing System, looking in and looking out, determining which children to refer to Children's Hearings and which to divert.

The Reporter is a curious hybrid. He/she is a local authority official and yet the Regional Reporter can be dismissed only by the authority of the Secretary of State for Scotland. A knowledge of law is required to assess evidence upon which a referral is made and/or Court work arising out of Children's Hearings, yet social assessment skills and a knowledge of family dynamics is crucial to help the Reporter in the vital decision making of determining whether a child may be in need of compulsory measures of care.

It is vital for the dynamics of the Hearing System that the Reporter is not seen as a remote bureaucratic official. Agencies should feel comfortable in referring appropriate cases to the Reporter and be able to trust the Reporter with the fullest possible information on children to assist his decision making. An increasing amount of the Reporter's workload is therefore concentrated on building up links with local agencies, involving themselves in training and meeting Headteachers and Guidance staff from local schools.

The Reporter's discretion is a key point of the system. Kilbrandon had identified the large number of children appearing in Juvenile Courts unnecessarily, swallowing up large amounts of time and resources. Reporters have recognised the importance of the principle of minimal intervention, looking at alternatives to compulsory measures of care such as voluntary assistance from the Social Work Department and encouraging parents to exercise their authority to resolve whatever problems are being presented by an individual child. National statistics demonstrate that only about 40% of referrals overall end up being referred to a Children's Hearing. It is interesting to contrast this figure with the percentage of children referred to Children's Hearings on the basis of failure to attend school regularly without reasonable excuse - 61%. Clearly, Reporters are referring far more children under this ground. This may be an indication of how serious the problem has become before it is referred to the Reporter or less charitably, it may be an indication of the lack of alternative, imaginative disposals available to the Reporter other than referring to a Children's Hearing.

Grounds of referral

The grounds upon which a child may be referred to a Children's Hearing are as follows: (1)

- a) that the child is beyond the control of his parents;
- b) that the child is falling into bad associations or is exposed to moral danger;
- c) that lack of parental care is likely to cause him unnecessary suffering or to seriously impair his health or development;
- d) any of the offences mentioned in Schedule 1 to the Criminal Procedure (Scotland) Act 1975 have been committed in respect of him or in respect of a child who is a member of the same household;
  - dd) that the child is, or is likely to become, a member of the same household as a person who has committed any of the offences mentioned in Schedule 1 to the Criminal (Procedure) Scotland Act 1975;
- e) that the child, being a female, is a member of the same household as a female in respect of whom an offence which constitutes the crime of incest has been committed by a member of that household;
- f) that the child has failed to attend school regularly without reasonable excuse;
- g) that the child has committed an offence;
  - gg) that the child has misused a volatile substance by deliberately inhaling other than for medicinal purposes that substance's vapour; (ie solvent abuse)
- h) that he/she is a child whose case has been referred to a Children's Hearing following a transfer from England or Wales;
- i) that the child is in the care of the local authority and his/her behaviour is such that special measures are needed for his adequate care and control (ie. in need of secure accommodation).

(An offence mentioned in Schedule 1 is an offence involving physical or sexual abuse or neglect most commonly).

The main ground of referral to a children's Hearing which concerns a problem at school is Section 32(2)(f) where a child is alleged to have failed to attend school regularly without reasonable excuse. Kilbrandon identified only 35 children committed to residential care as a result of truancy under the former Juvenile Court system. One suspects that the statistic is as misleading as current figures for referrals to the Reporter where national statistics average attendance referrals as 8% of the total referrals received by Reporters in Scotland over a 10 year period. Investigation of a referral on other grounds may reveal behavioural or attendance problems at school, which can be an influential factor in leading to referral to a Children's Hearing.

The Pack Report recommended that persistent indiscipline in schools be made an additional ground of referral to a Children's Hearing. Much to the relief of most Reporters, this recommendation was never enacted, partly in recognition of the problems of legal definition, partially in recognition that compulsory measures of care were not necessarily the answer to such problems.

However, there are cases where evidence of behavioural problems demonstrated by a pupil at school may be of relevance in helping to establish grounds of referral alleging a child to be beyond parental control. In such cases, evidence that such behaviour exists beyond the school to both home and the community would normally be essential.

One of the major developments in the Hearing System has been the growth of referrals in the category of alleged child abuse - e.g. Lothian Region has experienced a 400% increase in such referrals over the last 10 years. The problems evident at school may be significant in prompting a referral - for instance several referrals have originated from concerns expressed by primary schools about children displaying highly sexualised behaviour, inappropriate for a child of a young age. Further investigation has led to grounds being established, either that the child has been the victim of sexual abuse and is therefore the victim of a Schedule 1 offence, or that the child is exposed to inappropriate behaviour either live or on video and is therefore in moral danger. Training programmes, such as that initiated in Lothian Region through the 'Feeling, Yes, Feeling No' programme have helped increase the awareness of schools in their skill at recognising such situations and their ability to take appropriate action.

Children's Hearings

The Reporter refers a child to a Children's Hearing where he/she believes the child may be in need of compulsory measures of care. The Children's Hearing comprises 3 members of the Regional Children's Panel and each Hearing must include one member of each sex. Each year advertisements appear in the media

Chapter 6

in September seeking new members of the Panel. In the early days of the system, a large number of Panel Members were recruited from the education field. Latterly, the need to produce a broad cross section of the community has been more clearly recognised so there is not quite the preponderance of teachers that once existed.

Whilst increased diversion by Reporters may have led to a decrease in the number of referrals considered by Children's Hearings since the early days of the system, this is more than counterbalanced by the enormous increase in the complexity of the cases referred. This has been recognised by the development of comprehensive training for Panel Members which, on one hand creates an extra burden of time for already hard pressed volunteers but, on the other hand, has helped in the development of the many skills which are evident in the functioning of Children's Hearings today. One particularly crucial dynamic of the System which is often misinterpreted by those with little experience of the System, is the relationship between the Reporter and Panel Members and their very different functions. Once within the forum of the Children's Hearing, the Reporter has no influence on the decision of the Children's Hearing which is very much the responsibility of the Panel Members. The role of the Reporter within the Hearing is limited to advice on points of law and procedure and taking a minute of the proceedings of the Hearing.

The title of this chapter highlights a tension which can exist in the decision making within the Hearing System between the responsibilities of the Reporter and/or the Children's Hearing on the one hand and of the school on the other. As already stated, the focus of the Hearing System is on the needs and best interests of the individual child. Schools have a wider focus, taking account not only of the interests of the individual child, but also of the welfare of their institution as a whole. Action may be urged in relation to an individual child because of the effects his behaviour may be having on his or her fellow pupils, and the extent to which perceived lack of action may inflame such. A school may have justifiable concern over a child's behaviour and the detrimental effect this may have on the overall running of the school in terms of use of staff time and distraction of other pupils. That may influence a belief in the need for an alternative course of action such as residential schooling.

However, the Hearing need to be satisfied not only that the current care and education arrangements for a child are not appropriate, but that an alternative would be better. If a child is malfunctioning at day school but is not in trouble at home or in the community, the Hearing may be loth to consider removing a child from home. For instance in Lothian Region guidelines have been developed under Youth Strategy but no child should be recommended for residential care unless:

a) he/she has no home (including a substitute home) in the community which can with appropriate support provide an adequate degree of control or care, or
b) he/she is at risk to himself/herself or others in the community, or
c) he/she has medical, psychiatric or special educational needs which can only be dealt with in a residential context, and
d) it is in the child's best interests which cannot be met in any other way.

Problems are particularly encountered where a child is in his or her last year of schooling, especially when approaching their last term. Reporters are often reluctant to refer a child who is already in his last term of schooling as being in need of compulsory measure of care. Even where referral is made to Children's Hearing on the grounds of failure to attend school the actions which a Children's Hearing can take may be limited, especially where constructive benefits of a return to school are realistically acknowledged to be limited to a mark in a register and where alternatives are either not available or are judged not to be any better for the child. Kilbrandon's stress on the need for early action on a problem may be appropriately borne in mind to prevent late referral of children with long established school attendance problems.

The provision of informative and accurate reports is crucial to the functioning of the Children's Hearing and its decision making. The law requires reports to be available to Panel Members 3 clear days before the Hearing in order that they have time to digest the necessary information (2). The growth of the guidance system and the strengthening of relationships between Reporters and school staff has led to a greater understanding of the type of information required in reports, both in terms of substance and quality. There is less evidence now of the unsubstantiated hearsay information or of remarks bordering on the libellous, such as 'this boy is an inveterate liar and if he didn't commit this theft somebody else in his family did'.

The Hearing Members are interested in the complete picture of an individual child based on concrete facts and constructive comment. It can be easy to concentrate on the negative, as the following comment from a recent school report reveals:

'We have no relevant information to give you about John as we have received no adverse comments on his behaviour'.

Perhaps it should be emphasised that there is as much interest in positive as negative!

Research has demonstrated that the school's input is a crucial aspect of the Children's Hearing's decision making (Martin, Fox & Murray 1981). In 91% of the cases studied, schooling featured as a main topic of discussion while 31% of the children interviewed identified schools as especially influential to Panel Members in their decision making. This highlights the need for further development of appropriate training for guidance staff in their work with Children's Hearings and in particular in report writing.

The law also requires the Chairman of the Hearing to give families the substance of any report which may be material to the Hearing's decision unless any particular information is detrimental to the interests of the child to be revealed (3). Furthermore, if there is an Appeal against the decision of a Children's Hearing (4), the Sheriff will receive copies of all reports available to the Hearing and is entitled to question any writer of a report on its content. These laws underline the need for accuracy of information without, hopefully, inhibiting the breadth of it. Recent legislation governing the right to access of information has already created a climate where agencies, including some schools, are more inclined to share their reports openly with families prior to Hearings. Such openness can only be beneficial to the System, the conduct of the Children's Hearing and its decision making.

In practice there is wide divergence, both among schools and between regions, regarding the attendance of teachers at Children's Hearings. The Chairman of the Hearing has a legal duty to allow anybody in whose presence would be helpful to the Hearing (5) and where a child's school problems are being discussed it is helpful to have a teacher who knows the child, in particular his Guidance teacher, present. Experience in Lothian Region has been of teachers attending with great regularity and of such attendance being especially supportive to a child in the many cases where a close relationship exists between teacher and child and indeed, between parent and teacher. Attendance at a Hearing also enables a Hearing to delve more deeply, both into the content of the school report and into what further resources an individual school may have to offer a child in terms of support, which may prevent the need for looking at alternative resources. The absence of a teacher at a Children's Hearing may be an enormous block to appropriate consideration where the reason for referral relates to a school problem.

There are, however, occasions when the Chairman of the Hearing has to be mindful of the legal provision requiring him/her to keep members at a Hearing to a minimum (6) and which may mean the teacher is only present for part of a Hearing e.g. where there are large numbers present at the Hearing or where there are particular issues being discussed which it is considered would be best discussed with a minimum present.

Sheriff Court involvement

Where a referral is made to a Children's Hearing, the child and parent have the right to agree or disagree with the grounds upon which a referral has been made (7). In the event of a denial of the grounds, a Children's Hearing is not a Court of law, so cannot hear evidence in relation to the proof of those grounds. The Reporter will therefore be instructed to make an application to the Sheriff Court, unless the Hearing decides to discharge the referral. The Sheriff will hear the case presented by the Reporter, including relevant witnesses, and a child and parent may at this stage either jointly or separately be legally represented by a Solicitor who can present their case.

Applications are heard in private, usually either in the Sheriff's Chambers or a more informal Civil Court, away from the chaos of the Criminal Courts. The Sheriff and Lawyers make a bold gesture in recognition of what is intended to be a more informal atmosphere by dispensing with wearing their traditional wigs and gowns, but in all other respects this is a formal legal setting subject to normal rules of advocacy and evidence.

The majority of such cases go unreported and it is only where one of the parties believes that the Sheriff has erred on a point of law in his judgement that an appeal can be made to the Court of Session (8) where the opportunity may be created for defining case law and where there is more chance of the case being formally reported.

An appeal to the Court of Session can be a cumbersome process, especially in terms of time. I was involved in one case several years ago where a referral was made to a Children's Hearing in respect of two boys who allegedly had failed to attend school regularly without reasonable excuse. The grounds referred to a period of time covering only 2 weeks and were denied by both children and their parents. Their solicitor contested the grounds at the Sheriff Court on the basis that the 2 weeks were not sufficient to constitute 'regular' non attendance. The Sheriff upheld the grounds and remitted the case back to a Children's Hearing.

An appeal was made by Stated Case to the Court of Session by the family's solicitor. The appeal took 6 months to be heard. In the meantime the boys' cases had been considered by a Children's Hearing on the basis of the remit from the Sheriff Court and the referrals discharged. Both parties were still keen for the appeal to be heard, which gave an opportunity to obtain an authoritative ruling on an important point of the grounds of referral, but the court on hearing the case had been disposed of, literally threw their papers in the air muttering about 'waste of time' and 'bureaucratic minor officials' and we are still none the wiser on what constitutes 'regularly'. However there has been recent evidence of cases considered timeously by the Court of Session and often with beneficial effect to the clarification of controversial points of law.

It is clear from cases where parents have been prosecuted for failing to ensure their child's school attendance that production of a signed Headteacher's certificate will be sufficient to transfer the burden of proof to the child and parents in establishing that there was a reasonable excuse for the absences (9). English cases which are not binding on Scottish law but tend to be highly persuasive established that a parent's illness is not a reasonable excuse for a child's regular absence from school (10) and that absence for part of the school day is a failure in regular school attendance (11).

Most case law in existence is based on situations where parents are being prosecuted under the Education (Scotland) Act and while it may often be logical to assume that the same provisions apply to applications from Children's Hearings, this may often not be the case.

For instance, under the Education Act where a child is excluded from school for misconduct, the subsequent period of absence can be termed as without reasonable excuse. In an unreported case, D v Kennedy in 1987, the Court of Session stated clearly that that this reasoning cannot automatically be applied as covering referrals from Children's Hearings under the Social Work (Scotland) Act as well. Thus the mere fact that a child had been prevented from attending school by reason of exclusion based on misconduct is not sufficient to establish grounds of referral to a Children's Hearing alleging failure to attend school. The Court reserved opinion on the outcome had evidence of the misconduct been produced, but it appears likely that that would have been sufficient to establish 'without reasonable excuse'.

In that particular case, the attendance period in question ran from December 1985 to March 1986 and the original Children's Hearing was held in June 1986. The judgement from the Court of Session was dated October 1987. The child was due to leave school two months later!

The future

The Children's Hearing System has been used over the years as a focus to bring professional agencies together in tackling the problems of a child at school. Overworked social work departments, faced with multiple referrals in child abuse, are not able to give the same priority to children where problems may essentially appear school-based and indeed many in the profession have debated in the past whether they should have a role at all. It is easy under pressure of work to forget Kilbrandon's statement of truancy being a manifestation of problems at home. Schools, on the other hand, often see social work departments as dumping grounds for their 'failures' and have found it difficult in the past to recognise their ongoing duty towards the child.

Recent developments have brought the professions closer together and ironically, have come closer to recognising the rationale behind Kilbrandon's proposal for a Department of Social Education. Youth Strategy in Lothian has fostered good working relationships between social work and education in areas where none existed before. Such work can and has diverted children away from legal proceedings or provided constructive alternatives to residential care.

On a smaller scale, Wester Hailes Education Centre was responsible for creating the Co-ordinating Committee on Youth - a forum for all child oriented agencies covering the Wester Hailes area of Edinburgh such as Social Work Department, Police, local Youth Clubs, the Reporter and the Schools. The group met on a monthly basis and was able to look at joint initiatives in tackling issues arising for young people in the area - eg. racism, gang warfare, youth facilities for under-resources parts of the area, and support systems for those about to leave school. The creation and expansion of such initiatives is crucial in allowing Reporters to use their discretion imaginatively and appropriately when not referring to a Children's Hearing and can also lead to more substance to the content of home supervision requirements made by Children's Hearings.

In terms of the development of the law, in February 1988 the Secretary of State for Scotland commissioned a Review of Child Care Law in Scotland and its final Report was published in October 1990. The Report explored the relationship between Education and the Hearing System and the question was posed as to whether the grounds of failure to attend school regularly without reasonable excuse should be abolished on the basis that such cases are not indicative of a need for compulsory measures of care but rather as 'a school problem'. However, consultation and further deliberation led the Review to recommend the grounds' retention on the basis that:

'There are occasions when a child's failure to attend school is essential to a serious family problem which can be assisted by intervention. On such occasions failure to attend school may be the only problem which manifests itself in a child's behaviour. It would not be helpful to generalise the problem under another ground such as 'beyond control' or 'neglect' which might be misleading and to a degree, unfair. Retention of the existing ground provides a clear focus for referral upon which other wider, more underlying problems may be explored'.

The Review was, however, anxious to promote greater education involvement in the Children's Hearing System and recommended that, 'Children's Hearings should have access to the full range of local authority resources for children who reject normal schooling'.

That recommendation was based in part on a study by the Children's Panel

Chapter 6

Chairmen's Group which highlighted the difficulties for Panel Members' decision making caused by a lack of resources in general, including in the education field.

It is not absolutely clear how the Review's recommendation will assist that very real difficulty. Experience suggests that the root cause does not lie in the unwillingness of the Education Department to make existing resources available for use in disposals by Children's Hearings - rather it lies in stark reality that the full range of local authority resources for children who reject normal school is very limited. The notion that bringing this provision into law by itself will provide dramatic change needs to be questioned.

However, if such a provision is implemented it may contribute to further developing the current climate which recognises that children in trouble cannot easily be compartmentalised into sections exclusive to one agency. It could also highlight that the education profession is a core ingredient of the Children's Hearing System, with an essential role in helping the identification of what is in the best interests of a child. It is appropriate to end with the concluding paragraph from Kilbrandon -

> 'From the earliest age of understanding, every child finds himself part of a given family and a given environment - factors which are beyond his or society's power to control. During childhood the child is subject to influences of home and school. Where these have fallen short or failed, the precise means by which the special needs of this minority of children are brought to light are equally largely fortuitous. Individual needs may at this stage differ in degree but scarcely in essential character, and such children may be said at present to be, more than most, in a real and special sense 'hostages to fortune'. The time has come, we believe, when society may reasonably be expected so to organise its affairs as to reduce the arbitrary effects of what is still too often a haphazard detection process; and consequently to extend to this minority of children within a sustained and continuing discipline of social education, the measures which their needs dictate and of which they have hitherto been too often deprived'. (1964)

Notes

1. Section 32(2) Social Work (Scotland) Act 1968.

2. Rule 6. Children's Hearings (Scotland) Rules 1986.

3. Rule 19(3) Children's Hearings (Scotland) Rules 1986.

4. Section 49 Social Work (Scotland) Act 1968.

5. Rule 14(d) Children's Hearings (Scotland) Act 1986.

6. Section 35(2) Social Work (Scotland) Act 1968.

7. Section 42 Social Work (Scotland) Act 1968.

8. Section 50 Social Work (Scotland) Act 1968.

9. Kennedy v Clark 1970, SLT 260.

10. Jenkins v Howells 1961, 1 AU ER 218.

11. Hinchley v Rankin 1961, 1 All ER 692.

Chapter 6

References

Bruce, N & Spencer, J (1976). *Face to Face with Families: A Report on the Children's Panels in Scotland.* Macdonald.

Martin, F M, Fox S J & Murray, K (1981). *Children Out of Court.* Scottish Academic Press.

SED (1977). *Truancy and Indidiscipline in Schools. (The Pack Report).*

Scottish Office (1964). *Report on Children' & Young Persons. Cmmd. No. 2306 (The Kilbrandon Report).*

Scottish Office (1991). *Review of Child Care Law in Scotland.*

Chapter 7

Panmure House School Groups: One Approach to Dealing with Young People's Schooling Difficulties

Dave Simpson

For some time now there has been a gradual recognition that, to deal effectively and meaningfully with young people who are experiencing difficulties with their secondary schooling, a joint approach from both social work and education is a major prerequisite. By adopting and utilising the differing skills and techniques which both professions can offer, a valuable service can be given to such young people. The notion of joint work has long been recognised by the staff and managers of Panmure House.

Rightly, educationalists began to adopt and work to the principle that, ideally, young people having such difficulties should be dealt with within the confines of their local school. The Pack Report gave such a principle considerable emphasis and schools began to set up their own special units, where their young people could be offered some period of specialised educational provision.

To fully consider the line of argument that certain youngsters need a more specialist educational support, we need first to look at the whole area of specialist educational provision of which the Day Unit is a part. By the time the Pack Committee was set up in 1973 to look at the problems of truancy and indiscipline in Scotland, a handful of day unit type responses to the problems of certain pupils had already been inaugurated. The notion prevalent at that time, and indeed continued by Pack, was one of separation. At the risk of over-simplifying, the principle operating through much of this line of thinking was that, if we could set up separate facilities for pupils with difficulties, this would be in their long term interests and in the interests of schools where learning could proceed without interruption from those in difficulty.

Much of the response to the Pack Report, together with the weight of the view of the Warnock Committee (1978) on special education needs expresses an opposing view of integration. Interest is refocussed on schools and on how they can cater within their own structure for differing pupil's needs. Schools, certainly in Lothian, where great emphasis is attached to their Youth Strategy principles, are being encouraged to change their structure in order to accommodate the educational needs of most, if not all, the children in their catchment areas.

We at Panmure would concur with much of the reaction to the Pack Report and many of the sentiments expressed by Warnock on the responsibility of schools

Chapter 7

to first seek solutions within the confines of their own school to their own educational problems. Indeed, over the past few years there has been a dramatic shift in the problems of dealing with such young people within the local provision. Many factors have contributed to this change in the scale and nature of the problems. Increasingly, more young people are becoming disillusioned with their schools, thus exacerbating the issues and dilemmas the schools themselves are facing. Encouragingly, educationalists themselves have seized the opportunity provided by this crisis to take a long hard look at the nature of the curriculum. Munn and Dunning proposals, TVEI, the introduction of Standard grades and SCOTVEC modules are major steps in the re-thinking of secondary school provision.

Having said this, there exists a category of young people whose needs are best met within a centre based and more specialised setting. Such pupils need, as an educational priority, a measure of attention in the area of their social and emotional development which can only be offered by a joint approach from Social Work and Education Departments.

Before listing our aims and objectives it would be worthwhile to look at the causes of disruptive and unco-operative behaviour in schools. Individual insecurity and low self-image have been advanced as links in this chain of causality. Whatever further inter-connected links may be recognised - inadequate or interrupted parenting, housing, nutritional and employment deficiencies - the argument is that the problem demands an intervention based on an element of increased individual supports.

Without these, such damaged young people will fail to grow in any direction, other than that of continuing and deepening insecurity leading to self-effacement and despair. Far from benefiting from exposure to school, teachers, social workers and even peer group, these pupils find that social or educational interaction merely confuses them and continues the self-fulfilling cycle of non-achievement.

The development of the School Unit has its roots in the implementation of Lothian Region's Youth Strategy. It is only through the enterprise shown by the Education and Social Work Departments in jointly investing in such a scheme, that work in this area has been possible. The expansion of Youth Strategy into both Primary and Secondary sectors and the call for joint training is the beginning of a healthy sharing in common issues by both Departments.

The Youth Strategy initiatives have stimulated the development of imaginative and creative in-schools strategies geared towards meeting the needs of all young people. Our initial interest in developing the School Unit stemmed from our experience of work with schools and an awareness that a minority of young people fell outwith the then existing range of resources. They required a different and more intensive type of experience than schools could offer. The School Unit works directly with these young people while they remain on their own school roll. Strong working links with Secondary school staff are essential to ease the young person's return to mainstream schooling. Groupwork, learning support, general subject work, counselling and family work are also essential components of the work of the School Unit. In addition we offer support and advice to individuals and other agencies concerned with maintaining young people in their own community and their own school.

The school support provision based at Panmure House has provided three major elements of intervention. First, from its position of detachment from any local school, Panmure House has provided an alternative context for these youngsters whose experience of adults and peers alike has been negative. Although such a break is not appropriate for all pupils, it is desirable for some. Second, as part of the educational programme young people have an experience of groupwork. Third, it can offer an intensive type of relationship with adults different from that in school.

The general aims of the School Unit are as follows:

1. To provide a resource which is in line with the Principles of Lothian Region's Youth Strategy and which attempts to meet the educational, social and emotional needs of young people.
2. To provide an environment and learning experience which will encourage young people to feel valued and considered as worthwhile individuals.
3. To provide a setting where social work and education staff can share observations and participate in joint working practice with young people and their families.
4. To provide an opportunity for young people to return to mainstream education.
5. To provide a varied but well organised and structured programme which combines social work and educational methods.

Whilst acknowledging that Panmure House is an off-site unit and thus superficially seems to be following the Pack Model, the philosophy that underpins our work is more akin to Warnock et al. This is clearly seen in our expectations that schools:

- own their responsibilities by allowing referred pupils to remain on parent school's roll
- provide clear re-entry routes through offering morning or afternoon provision as appropriate

Chapter 7

- provide and assess pupil's work
- work towards reintegration from the outset.

These points will be touched upon and explored in greater detail in the later part of this chapter.

The groupwork programme offered to young people is aimed at encouraging an awareness of individual worth and the development of essential social skills. A variety of activities, using a range of exercises and techniques enables the creation of an atmosphere of trust among group members which, in turn, has allowed an exploration of the difficulties being experienced by the young people in their daily lives.

There are several reasons why groupwork is considered a useful method in working with young people. The central one is that a group is productive because it is a shared experience between participants, (including adults). Being part of a group with shared difficulties in itself reduces isolation. Being part of a group which is supportive provides a stable base for individuals to take risks and either achieve or fail in the knowledge that there will be peers and adults around who will maintain their commitment and support. In such an environment the individuals self perceptions can be constructively challenged.

The School Unit can provide a different type of adult/child relationship to that generally found in mainstream schools. This is based partly on the high adult/young person ratio, but the main element of this "difference" is without doubt the quality of the relationship which can be built between adult and young person in this particular setting.

Often for the first time in a young person's life he or she can relate to an adult who offers a consistent degree of openness, warmth and challenge. A good trusting relationship can then be used as the basis for the young person's development, both in an educational and social sense.

Within a context of developing responsibility, young people are encouraged to participate in decisions which affect themselves and the whole group. Relationships are developed which, though directive, are not rejecting; which are private without being secretive; and which are sympathetic without being collusive. Such relationships are necessary because change in the self perception of young people is difficult without a degree of trust in adults and adult authority. The process of accepting responsibility and of decision making itself, both at personal and group levels, is a process of increasing personal investment in any decisions reached and an increased awareness of the implications of such decisions.

Strategies for Learning

The programme offered to young people attending Panmure House School Unit is under constant review and is subject to change at frequent intervals. Individual programmes are tailored to particular needs. This is an area which requires negotiation between the young person, their school and Panmure House. There are as many individual programmes as there are young people attending Panmure House and they range from those which allow young people to return to their base school and be presented for Standard grades, to those designed to deal with basic problems in numeracy and literacy. In all cases the co-operation and help we have had from base schools has been of the highest order.

The wide variations in educational achievement and experience found among the Unit's pupils means, inevitably, that the ideal of pupils working largely with packages from their mainstream schools is not always completely feasible. Long term absences and the disruption to their timetable caused by their attendance at the Centre can make the provision of these packages very difficult. The style of the Standard Grade and the linear nature of some subjects also militates against this happening in some cases.

However, there are successful examples of high levels of support from mainstream staff enabling pupils to follow, as much as is possible, the curriculum of their mainstream classmates. An instance of this, perhaps, would be in the organisation of a General Science course so that practical work is done in school and theory in Panmure.

The fact remains, however, that for a number of the Centre's pupils, for varying reasons, the bulk of their educational provision and maybe chances of qualifications, will be instituted by the Centre's staff. For these, and indeed all the pupils, the use of SCOTVEC modules is being developed, the Centre having previously gained SCOTVEC accreditation. The thinking behind this partly reflects the fact that, particularly in the area of PSD, the modular courses are virtually a formalisation of work already being undertaken in the Centre, as in Life and Work and Community Involvement, whilst Work Experience and Managing your Money are of obvious support to pupils in their final months before leaving school.

Staff are aware of the dangers of attempting to modularise too widely and, as in any other area of the provision, pupils will only undertake modules that have direct relevance to them. However, parts of modules and various combinations will continue to be used, where appropriate, even when not leading to formal qualifications. In this area Leisure and Recreation, Media Studies and Residential Experience are obviously of great use. Third and fourth year pupils, whose mainstream schooling experience makes the following of Standard Grade Maths or English courses difficult, have the option of Core Maths and Communications modules.

However, as initially stated, flexibility is the keynote - not only in the service given to each pupil but also in the use that is made of resources. It is understood that, whilst undertaking modular, or modular type courses, the pupils will make full use of the resources available within Panmure House, including Computing, Photography, Drama, Art and Crafts, Music and Video. Staff are strongly against too narrow a definition of what constitutes educational provision. The expansion in the use of Modules achieves a number of objectives. As stated, it formalises the type of Personal and Social Development work already being done by pupils, thus making it more easily demonstrable to other agencies or employers and, importantly, it provides an added opportunity for the Centre's pupils to gain qualifications, despite a disrupted mainstream schooling. This development is, of course, part of the overall remit of reintegration but will serve particularly well the needs of those pupils who experience difficulty in achieving complete reintegration. For those pupils who effectively have to leave school from the Centre, it provides a service they have not, for a variety of reasons, been able to gain from mainstream. Its flexibility lends itself to individual and appropriate provision for each pupil.

Aside from this main area of development, the staff of the Centre remain committed to continually improving the education provision in a general sense by upgrading resources; maintaining links with colleagues and departments in mainstream, as well as the Advisory Service; meeting regularly with staff involved at present in similar work, with a view to joint training projects; and seeking to make full use of Panmure House staff skills and resources. it is clear that the provision must continue to develop and reflect the needs of the pupils who attend the Centre at present and will in the future. As the Centre widens the number of schools with which it works, more resources and ideas become available from new staff contacts and these contribute to the building up of a bank of material within the Centre.

Present experience indicates that perhaps the next development might well be in the area of strengthening the existing links with F.E. Colleges so that the service offered to pupils in their last few months of schooling can be further expanded.

To summarise, pupils within the Centre can expect to experience a balance between the social and academic provision. Staff believe that there is integration of these two areas. Mainstream work is undertaken on the basis of regular contact with school guidance and subject staff: a number of modules are available, where appropriate, and may be taken formally or without seeking full certification: full use of methods within the Creative and Aesthetic sphere is encouraged in all areas of the provision. The Centre attempts to provide each pupil with the educational experience which is of most relevance and appropriacy. To do this it relies on close working with the pupil and family, sharing of ideas within the staff team and the support and co-operation of the mainstream school and outside agencies.

No matter what the programme comprises, it is governed by the following principles:

1. *Recognition of Achievement*

Young people referred to Panmure House will generally be seen by agencies and themselves to have failed within the school setting. The educational programme should, therefore, allow each person to achieve according to their abilities. For some this will, initially, simply be regular attendance at Panmure House. Encouragement has to be given at all levels in social as well as academic learning. For many young people referred, their academic potential will only be realised when emotional needs are met.

2. *The Curriculum Should be Attractive*

The young people who attend Panmure House School Unit have been unable, for a variety of reasons, to use constructively what the mainstream school has offered them.

Many of our young people need assistance with basic learning skills and are on individual programmes. These programmes relate to personal preferences, motivation, ability and specific needs. Young people need encouragement to define their own needs so the curriculum offered must be of interest and relevance. Our main aim is for the young people to feel positively involved in their own learning. Such an approach has helped young people to develop confidence in themselves and, as a result, they are more able to engage positively and constructively in their education.

3. *Schools maintain responsibility for their Young People*

All young people who attend the School Unit are referred via the School Liaison Groups. To date, all schools have co-operated with agreed contracts. Unit staff are having increasing contact with Secondary Schools as arrangements for part-time attendance at the base school and assistance with teaching programmes are required. It is vital that Secondary School staff are involved in all discussions re the young person's education. It is also important that information known at senior level is shared with Heads of Department and Subject Teachers.

So far, our experience has been positive although some issues have called for further consideration, eg. both ourselves and schools quickly realised that a system offering dual attendance was open to abuse and needed to be more closely monitored. A new system has been set up and is now working effectively. A further example is that, in order to re-establish young people within their own school, more of the same is not appropriate, since it has already failed, therefore, a more imaginative use of curriculum is needed. It makes sense that if the work at the school unit is deemed successful, then we have to try to transplant successful elements - whether they be relationships, groupwork or alternative education programmes - back into mainstream school.

Our own internal research has shown that the young people who have attended the School Unit have, generally, achieved something. For some young people, the reality of returning to full-time mainstream education has not been realised. It has nevertheless been possible to make use of established links towards integration into the wider society, ie. employment, college courses, community education, etc.

4.   *Promoting Change in School*

The above is probably the key to the success of Lothian Region's Youth Strategy. Unless schools can be persuaded to adopt a more flexible way of encouraging young people to take responsibility for their own learning, it is difficult to see how some young people will maintain themselves at school. Promotion of change is already being attempted through employment of Youth Strategy teachers and groupworkers with some visible signs of success. However, this type of work could be further enhanced by allowing school unit staff to work more closely with base schools. This would allow an exchange of ideas on which strategies have been tried and how effective or ineffective they have been. It could further encourage school staff in their attempts to develop new strategies and give Panmure House staff access to In-School In-Service Programmes.

Family Work

Work with families of young people attending at Panmure House is seen as an integral part of the service offered by the Unit. To succeed in this, it is important to establish good relationships based on understanding and trust. We attempt to develop these relationships by meeting parents at the first stage of referral and by maintaining contact throughout the young person's career at Panmure House.

This process begins when the initial 'Home Visit' is made to assess a young person's suitability for a place at Panmure House and is followed up by parental involvement in the pre-admission meeting and in reviews. All meetings and reviews held within Panmure House have been attended by either one or in some cases both parents. The co-operation we have received from the parents has been extremely good and therefore worth noting, as many of these parents have previously been described as, for example, unresponsive.

The main task of our work with families has been to build relationships. Through this it has been possible to challenge the sometimes negative attitudes of the family to formal education and to begin to influence and challenge impressions which have often been based on the experience of the parent, as child and pupil. By involving parents more fully in the decisions regarding their child's education it has, in many cases, been possible to alter some of the parental attitudes to school based education. Generally this has been beneficial for the young person and family's understanding of each other. There are instances where such is not the case but a supportive and caring attitude toward the family, coupled with a degree of firmness as to the importance of regular attendance, has nonetheless continued to show encouraging results.

Regular contact with families has taken place either through home visits or by telephone, should immediate contact be necessary, eg. with medical appointments, illness. Obviously the amount of family contact is determined by either the young person or their families needs and varies accordingly. In the event of crisis work being required priority is given to carrying this out.

In looking back over the past two years it appears that the objective of offering a service to young people both in the Unit and at home has been realised. This is confirmed by the excellent working relationship we have with many of the parents of young people attending the Unit. Family work has also involved us in joint work with area team Social Workers, regular attendances at Children's Hearing, Child Care Reviews and Assessment Meetings.

Summary

The Panmure House School Unit is a place of caring and support for pupils and school staff alike. It provides an extended opportunity for pupils 'lost' in the system, for whatever reason, to take a long look at themselves in a 'safe' though challenging environment. It asks the questions which need to be addressed and has a staff with the expertise to help the youngsters find and cope with the answers.

The young people who attend Panmure House are with us because their recent school records have been characterised by frequent truancy and/or disruptive behaviour. Many hold a cynical attitude towards school, an antipathy towards learning and have a poor self image. The difficulties encountered in the learning context, such as disruptive, withdrawn or unco-operative behaviour often have their origin in individual or family insecurity. If such personal difficulties cannot be met, then clearly there is little hope for any advance in terms of educational progress. Such young people have a limited capacity to cope with even the known present. The prospect of the unknown, the future, or even a new chapter in a mathematics book must seem like a step into unimaginable darkness. Given such a view of the world, truancy, avoidance or the creation of diversions are obvious devices.

The main learning needs for these young people are growth in self worth and the development of trusting relationships and these can only be achieved by examining and coping with the sources of personal insecurities. This is not an easy task and in our view some young people will struggle even in the most supportive settings. However, these young people should not be abandoned. The existence of Centres, such as Panmure House, provide much needed breathing spaces for many young people, whilst at the same time allowing them to continue their educational development.

Much valuable experience has been gained over the last two years through a joint approach to working with young people. The existence of Youth Strategy Centres should not preclude, but rather assist, the development of school based facilities to meet the needs of their other young people. In this way Youth Strategy centres form just one part of a planned range of educational resources within Lothian Region, where young people may be afforded the opportunity to sustain or return to mainstream education.

Without exception every young person who has attended the School Unit over the past year has been given the opportunity to achieve the above aim. Some have been sustained on their school roll, a few have been returned to school but all have been supported through a critical phase in their educational careers. If success can be quantified in terms of attendance and commitment, then the School Unit has been effective. If it can be measured in growth, motivation and the self development of the young people worked with, then we have accomplished a great deal.

The Panmure House School Unit has been in operation for over two years and throughout that time has offered a direct service to schools and pupils in Edinburgh. Additionally, by emphasising a multi-disciplinary approach the Unit has helped the development of a partnership between social work and education departments in intervening in the lives of pupils who are failing to respond to current in-school strategies. As might be expected in any innovative development difficulties have been encountered but generally the work of the Unit can be regarded as a success.

The Unit - to quote Councillor Maginnis, Chairperson of Lothian Region's Education Committee, has

> 'blurred the distinction between mainstream and special education, creating structures which relieve individual guilt and replacing it with a shared responsibility between pupil, family, school and community. Changes are occurring and the process of developing in-school care strategies for all pupils is taking place.'

Although changes of this nature will always be surrounded by obstacles, we are equally committed to promoting this type of change. Our ambitions of establishing additional support systems to ensure all categories of pupils are being catered for are slowly but surely being realised.

References

SED (1977). *Truancy and Indiscipline in Schools (The Pack Report).*

HMSO (1978). *Special Educational Needs; Report of the Committee of Enquiry into the Education of Handicapped Children & Young People (The Warnock Report).*

Chapter 8

Neighbourhood Projects and the School
Barry Wilford

Introduction
This chapter is about youth/social work projects, that in addition to providing broad based youth work programmes to local young people, have also been centrally involved with the development and provision of specifically 'youth strategy' related programmes and activities, i.e., support for young people facing and/or posing difficulties in their schools and local communities. Naturally I am drawing heavily and directly from experience gained from the work done at the centre I manage, the Citadel Youth Centre, but also from a long aquaintance with the field and familiarity with the work of similar projects. It is I believe, representative of an approach to providing support and services to young people and their families which is replicated by other youth/social work projects in Lothian Region, and indeed throughout Scotland.

The term youth/social work is employed not to diminish the value of youth work but to emphasise the two professional disciplines that contribute to the practice of these projects. The contribution these projects make to school support systems is being increasingly acknowledged and encouraged, as examples of successful collaboration between schools and youth/social work projects proliferate.

Background
Neighbourhood youth/social work projects tend to be in the voluntary sector, managed by local community groups and supported and funded by one of the major child-centred charities or by the local authority. Staff are usually professionally qualified and may come from different training backgrounds, most commonly Youth and Community, Social Work or Education. They may be supported by teams of local part-time workers and volunteers.

In examples of good practice the programmes developed by these projects are invariably shaped and influenced by local issues and concerns, e.g. outreach work in an area where 'gangs' are congregating and fighting, or a health education group for young people abusing drugs, and developed to complement the services that are provided through the statutory sector, perhaps providing some that should be but are not, eg, a group work programme for young offenders. Inevitably being aware of the local 'landscape' and responding to it has lead these projects to place differing emphases on the range and substance of services they deliver.

Some have developed a broad preventative approach, with the emphasis on providing 'open' youth work programmes for all local young people, but also providing groupwork and counselling services to targeted groups of young people 'at risk'. Other projects have developed their programmes with an emphasis on groupwork delivered to young people referred by other agencies e.g., schools or the social work department, and some may offer a level of support to individual young people which effectively corresponds to the role of a supervising social worker.

The majority of projects attempt to achieve a balanced programme which responds directly and relevantly to the needs expressed by the local community: young people; parents; local community groups; and local agencies: schools; social work department; community education department; police; childrens hearing centre.

It is common for youth/social work projects supported by regional councils to be jointly funded by the Education (through Community Education) and Social Work departments. This underlines the expectation that the remit of such projects will fall somewhere between the Social Work, Education and Youth Work Services. It is therefore perhaps not surprising given the professional backgrounds of the project staff, and the sources of funding that many of the most highly developed and well established examples of interagency collaborative work providing support are to be found within the programmes developed by these projects.

Another important contributory factor in the development of their programmes for some of these projects was the formal endorsement of inter-agency action, to retain troubled and troublesome young people in their homes, schools and local communities through regional youth strategies.

The development of youth strategies in a sense 'legitimised' and raised the profile of existing examples of inter-agency work in this field, and by providing a positive environment and increasingly clear guidelines and frameworks in which to operate, encouraged new initiatives to develop. Although there is still some way to go in most of the regions that support youth strategies and few are without their critics, (some constructive - others less so!) Previously local arrangements between schools and youth/social work projects are increasingly being seen as part of coherent region wide responses to provide services to young people experiencing and/or posing problems within the school setting and in their communities.

What Do Youth/Social Work Projects Offer

Projects may employ a variety of methods and approaches in their work with young people at risk.

Chapter 8

Following is a short list:

Psycho-Dynamic Groupwork
Social Groupwork
Centre Based Youth Work
Outreach Work
Detached Work
Social Action
Activity Groups
Girls Work
Boys Work
Befriending
Work with Ethnic Minority Groups
Counselling
Supervision Groups
Truancy Groups
Excludee Groups

This list is by no means exhaustive and is entirely consistent with the expectations of funding bodies who look for creativity and innovation from a 'freed up' Voluntary Sector Project.

However for my purposes here I will represent the work as falling in three main areas.

1. 'Open' Youth Work Provision.
   i.e. Preventative and non-selective.
2. Groupwork - Targeted Intervention.
3. Keyworker
   i.e. A member of staff allocated responsibility to befriend, support and/or counsel a young person.

Following are three examples from our Project of how we use these approaches in relation to our work with local schools.

1. Citadel/Fort Primary School Project.
   'Open' Collaborative and Preventative work, linked to classwork, with a whole class of a local primary school.

2. Groupwork: With a group of disruptive and disaffected fourth year pupils.

3. Keyworker: Individual support offered to a young person experiencing difficulties by a member of the project staff.

1. Citadel/Fort Primary School Project
   April - June 1990

Introduction.
Citadel Youth Centre has for some time been committed to running groups, within Secondary Schools, for troubled and troublesome young people in need of extra support. The importance of such provision has been recognised by the Council's Youth Strategy policy which has recently advocated work in the primary school area in order to intervene at an earlier stage with children experiencing difficulties.

As a result of discussions between Fort Primary and the Citadel it was decided to target the primary 3 class to be involved in a pilot project throughout the Easter-Summer term. An application for material costs was approved through a Youth Strategy grant and the staffing needs were met by the Citadel and Fort Primary.

In the past the Citadel has run 3 'out of school' small groups in conjunction with the Fort which have proved, in the main, successful. The benefits of these groups, although discriminating positively in favour of pupils who needed extra support, were limited to those few. It was felt that by devising a method of working with the whole class, and with the teacher of P3, a larger number of children would be able to share experiences, which link directly with class work. It was hoped that experiences would be shared verbally and visually to encourage a sense of achievement, thus offering some children an opportunity to overcome their sense of failure, sometimes acquired in the classroom setting.

Staffing
   1 class teacher   - Fort Primary School
   2 Project Staff   - Citadel Youth Centre

Initially the staffing of the group was to consist of one member of Citadel staff and the class teacher, However the use of the video camera, for class back-up work and recording, meant that it would be more practicable to have two members of the Citadel staff involved. Since the class teacher was to be working directly with the groups out of school every week there was a need to provide teaching cover for the remainder of the class. This was provided through the commitment of the school and the willingness of the school staff to be flexible in order to cover.

The group

The class was split into three groups of 8, 8 and 7 children. These groups were of mixed sex and selected by the class teacher to provide a variety of abilities, qualities and behaviour. In preparation the staff had decided that balanced groups would lend themselves more to the aims of the project.

Each group on a weekly rota basis spent the morning outwith school on one of the trips/visits. the class teacher and project staff spent the morning with the group whilst the rest of the class remained in school. On return to school, if any issues were needing addressed, then this would be done during the lunch break.

The afternoon session was spent in class with the whole of P3 undertaking work relating to specific areas of the project.

Programme
Week 1 - Edinburgh Castle
Week 2 - Portobello Beach
Week 3 - Gorgie Farm and Fort Saughton
Week 4 - The Royal Botanic Gardens and Inverleith Park
Week 5 - Trip to Aberdour by Train (Over Forth Rail Bridge)
Week 6 - Gullane Beach
Week 7 - Gullane Beach
Week 9 - Visit to the Royal Highland Show (Complete Class)

In addition the staff group also went on a class summer outing to the Butterfly Farm and Vogrie Country Park.

The overall content of the programme attempted to provide a balance of interesting educational trips with recreational experiences which combined to capture the imagination and enthusiasm of the pupils. For example, Group 1's programme consisted of - Edinburgh Castle, Botanic Gardens, Gullane and Highland Show.

Without exception these sessions were looked forward to by the children - a combination of being out of school and exciting destinations probably accounts for this. The high staff/children ratio encouraged the children to continually ask questions (since they could rely on receiving some attention and an answer). We found that not only were the energetic children stimulated in a more positive direction, but also the normally quieter children felt confident enough to sustain a conversation, initially about the trip, and then about themselves.

The afternoon session in school.

The session after lunch began with the whole class watching the video recording of the morning's trip out. This gave the class a picture of the trip and always provided the class with considerable enjoyment. The video provided an important link between those in school and out of school, and managed to bring the children together as one big group for the afternoon's work component. It appeared that much story-telling and describing the mornings trips went on at lunch time in the playground. We also had many stories told within the class group.

Advantages of staff/pupil ratio.
The staff pupil ratio benefitted the children in a number of ways. It allowed the children individual attention from adults, thus contributing to the quality of relationship. The staff were able to focus on any particular problems an individual was experiencing in relation to his/her peer group, and have the time available to attempt to resolve this. Pupils had the opportunity to discuss their work individually or in groups, with staff, e.g., reading, writing, arts, crafts.

Through encouragement pupils appeared more confident and able to contribute to the whole class and its work, reflecting a sense of personal achievement, co-operation and general investment in the work and class group.

Working towards the group aims.
The staff, from the planning stages, recognised the need to create a warm and caring atmosphere in the group so as to help the children to develop the ability to relate to both adults and each other. This was achieved through a process of continual encouragemen to the children. In the early planning stages the staff discussed discipline issues and the possibility of differing expectations of behaviour. Through these issues being discussed at an early stage a commonalty of approach and a clear understanding of our aims were established.

Aims.
- i. To provide a range of positive, rewarding experiences and activities which otherwise are unlikely to be available.
- ii To enhance the children's quality of relationships with peers and adults through shared experiences in environments less formal than school.
- iii To encourage co-operative participation in recording and reporting back to classmates.
- iv To encourage the children's investments in school through use of exciting activities, recording, sharing and developing curricular areas.
- v To encourage a sense of achievement through school work and aid the transition from infant to junior departments.

Chapter 8

Many of the children within the target group, and indeed within the school experience disadvantage in their day to day lives because of their unstable home life, lack of encouragement or opportunity and a general background of deprivation.

A Morning Out to Aberdour Via the Forth Rail Bridge

Meeting to go on a trip.
The whole class is very excited even though two thirds of them are not going. There is lots of chat about great railway journeys of our time from those who have been on a train before, and great anticipation from those who haven't. For a surprisingly large number of children, this is their first train journey. Many children's stories of last time they were on a train relate to holidays, visits to relatives etc.

Mini-bus to station
Continuation of lots of chat between children and adults. The staff try to structure the conversation in an attempt to calm the group down a bit. "Spot the Herbie" game holds most of the childrens concentration.

Station.
The energetic kids are being kept a close eye on, the dangers of the station having been previously pointed out. The children are full of inquisitiveness, playing with telephones, looking in bins, climbing on seats and sliding on the slippy pavement slabs. Fortunately the train arrives, since interest has worn off in the arrival/departure board. Train arrives and kids unprompted couple up for the walk down the platform. They continually remind themselves, each other and the staff how dangerous platforms can be if you don't stay in twos or misbehave. A few venture to speculate the injuries one might receive if run over by a train.

Train
Usual scramble for seats, but all settle down quickly. Staff take up strategic positions e.g., beside a child sitting alone or with two particularly excited children. There is a brief lull in the general noise as the train starts. Noise resumes as children point out Edinburgh Castle, the Scott Monument, Princes Street Gardens, Burger King, where the squirrels live, railway workers, etc. Although there has been great excitement no stern or firm words have been necessary. Staff engage children, going round everyone talking either individually or in groups.

One of the main focuses of the day draws near - crossing the Forth Rail Bridge. Children take up positions with the best vantage point. Most are either standing or held steady by staff. The crossing creates a variety of responses from quiet approval to a barrage of questions - including 'what would it be like to fall off the bridge and into the water?' A couple of children stay sitting on staff's knees for the remainder of the journey. Other children make faces at a baby sitting nearby much to the baby's delight.

Beach
Arriving at Aberdour we make our way to the beach which is a ten minute walk. The weather is fine. The staff decide that the children can go into the water since there will be time to get dried before the train. Some children play by themselves, some paddle or play in the sand in twos and threes. The staff do not intervene. The children chop and change who they play with. All make their way to base camp as the call goes out for snack time. Chat continues throughout snack time, the children obviously enjoying the less formal setting and contact with their teacher as well as the attention of two other adults.

Children point out Edinburgh on the horizon and particularly visible points of Leith. Most of the rubbish from the snack is conscientiously put in the litter bag, they have done work in the class on rubbish and the environment!

Departure
Time to go and the usual tangle of lost socks, lost shoes, lost towels, knotted shoelaces, lost half eaten bags of crisps as well as one child who won't come out of the water, but there is still enough time to catch the train. Eventually we make our way, some children in front, others hopping at the back - a combination of walking and tying shoelaces simultaneously. One of the children needs some individual attention because he has had a memorable time and doesn't want to return to Edinburgh. The staff encourage those way behind to have a race and see if they can catch the children at the front. The improvised sounds of space shuttles, racing cars etc., fills the air. We arrive at the station, the children are excited and restless, they are encouraged by their teacher to recite poetry learned in class to the two other workers. Individual and group recitals follow with great enthusiasm. The train arrives and the return trip is spent chatting. A couple of the quieter children on the outward journey sit close to adults chatting, giggling and gently wrestling with them. Most of the children now gather round the adults.

On the mini-bus trip back to school the talk is about dinners and where the next visit will be to. General comments indicate the children have all enjoyed their morning out and look forward to the afternoon class work.

2. A Secondary School Leavers Group.
The purpose was to offer a useful and rewarding experience to ten fourth year students from a local secondary school who were approaching their final school term but were effectively 'disengaged' from the mainstream schooling experience.

This situation may have been due to the young persons' failure to attend school or the result of action taken by the school in response to unacceptable behaviour e.g. exclusion.

The programme offered was not to be presented as a full 'alternative' schooling experience, or as a means of encouraging re-integration (meaningless for this age group), but as a device to maintain contact with young people in danger of disappearing into an educational limbo. By attending this group the young person remained on the school role and could be encouraged to use school resources when appropriate, e.g. careers service, specifically useful classes.

Type of group.
The programme was broadly 'social education' with input to encourage social skills generally and specifically to provide support, encouragement and practical assistance in seeking appropriate employment or entrance to a training scheme. Other issues emerging through this programme were relationships with parents, housing, sexual identity, violence and aggression, health, use and abuse of drugs and use of leisure.

Methods employed included group and individual counselling, discussion, video, role play, special interest projects and access to outdoor adventure activities. A 'Social Groupwork" approach was used.

The group met in the centre one morning a week between 10.00 a.m. and 12.15 p.m , with occasional full day sessions to accommodate special trips and activities. Residential activities were negotiated by the young people and depended on the level of responsibility and commitment shown by them to make the group a positive experience.

Each session was staffed by two project staff and usually took place at the centre. Additional resources such as minibus, food, craft materials, camping equipment etc., were provided by the centre.

The sessions were recorded to:
i. Assist the development of the young people attending the group.
ii. Ensure the good practice of the workers.
iii To monitor the effectiveness of the scheme in attracting and working creatively with a group of 'disengaged' young people.

The programme lasted one school term.

3. Keyworker. A Case Study:
Diana Shaw was a pupil at a local primary school who was experiencing increasing difficulties in relating to her peer group and staff at the school. Her school work was also below average and was causing teaching staff some concern. An

appointment was made by the school for Diana and her mother to meet with the school doctor for a routine medical examination. The school doctor was concerned at Mrs Shaw's very negative reaction to an critical comments of Diana. The school therefore decided to refer Diana to the educational psychologist.

It was discovered that Mrs Shaw was also concerned about Diana but was indignant about the schools' observations of her criticism of her daughter. She found Diana to be moody and difficult to cope with. Her lack of social skills annoyed her, as did the fact that she wouldn't go out unless accompanied by her older sister.

The home situation was becoming strained and Diana was being blamed. There was also concern that Dianna would not cope well in secondary school.

Method of Referral.
The educational psychologist had mey with Diana and her mother on a number of occasions and felt that Diana would benefit from some positive social experiences. She felt that contact with the local youth project would be beneficial to Diana as it would help her build confidence and therefore enable her to have a more equal place in school and at home. Time out of the house would also lessen the tensions between Mr and Mrs Shaw who argued over the difficulties their daughter was experiencing.

Methods Employed.
Initial home visit to meet Diana and her mother in order to discuss the options available and to get and idea of the perceived problems. Mrs Shaw was most anxious to avoid her daughter being labelled as a 'problem'. However she was desperate for Diana to become 'more like other children'. Diana appeared comfortable and interested in what I said about the project and how she could become involved. During the visit it became apparent that there were difficulties in the relationship between Mr and Mrs Shaw, financial worries and demands on time through work. Diana was beginning to be 'scapegoated' within the family and her difficulties at school being blamed as the cause for other problems within the home. Decided to offer individual befriending; in order to discover more about Diana by engaging in social activities and individual assessment to discover more about her perceptions of home and school and the best ways of coping with them.

Open Youth Clubs; a gradual introduction to open youth clubs as an introduction to mixing with peers in a social setting.

Advocacy at Home; in order for Diana to communicate more effectively with her family.

Outcome of project involvement.
Befriending was taken slowly at Diana's own pace so we could get to know each other well. Diana was very keen to join in the Youth Clubs and eventually became confident enough to start in the Girls Club one evening a week with support from myself.

Introduction was a great success and within a short time Diana had become very involved and had built good relationships with the other girls.

Regular home visits during this time to consult with Mrs Shaw over Diana's progress, which was marked at home. She had surprised her mother by actually going out and 'playing' which had relieved some of the tensions in the household.

Older sister also joined club and attended Girls Club and mixed open night on Wednesdays. Diana was encouraged to attend but preferred the Girls Club which she also introduced to friends from school.

A number of residential week-ends throughout the summer sealed Diana's involvement and enjoyment with us. Family's concern over the move to secondary school greatly lessened.

General support throughout summer allowed preparation to be done for starting secondary school which has so far been a great success.

Present Situation.
Diana has now been involved with the Project for nine months and that time has seen her blossoming into a likeable, confident and sociable young girl. The family are far less critical of her and relationships have improved. Mrs Shaw is happy with the service the project has offered and all the children now attend the various youth clubs on offer.

Diana is much more confident in the school environment and feels better equipped to cope and take risks, as the initial risk of experiencing involvement in social settings has proved to be a rewarding one for her.

Conclusion
Workers in youth/social work projects enjoy many advantages over their colleagues in the statutory sector which contribute to their ability to deliver effective and relevant support to young people facing difficulties. Freed from departmental constraints project staff can negotiate directly with key school (and other agency) staff to create locally responsive services. Autonomy and the ability to implement decisions quickly encourage flexible and evolving programmes in line with local needs and circumstances.

Staff of youth/social work projects can concentrate all their energy and resources effectively to providing services to young people as they are (generally) free of the heavy burdens of statutory, administrative and curricular responsibilities carried by Social Workers, Educational Psychologists, Community Education Workers and Teachers. Being free of statutory responsibilities eases the process of befriending and relationship building between workers and young people as the disadvantage of being perceived in a controlling or authoritarian role is absent.

Youth Projects are usually sited in buildings which are designed and equipped to be attractive to young people, different areas encourage either stimulation and excitement, or provide comfortable rooms for discussion or counselling. Many schools, despite their size and resources, do not have a suitable area - comfortable, informal and free from outside disturbances for groupwork to take place. A neighbourhood project rarely has to work with more than one, two or three schools. This facilitates developing close working relationships with key staff and encourages quick and effective negotiation about individual cases and the development of school support services.

A neighbourhood project's contribution to community life through its 'open' programme and involvement in local issues can mean a readier and more trusting acceptance of offers of counselling and support by young people and parents. Project staff can contribute to effective decision making on the basis of familiarity with a local young person, issue, or school.

Naturally relationships between youth/social work projects and schools are not always harmonious. Confrontations and misunderstanding arise over individual young people and their treatment and issues such as welfare versus discipline or groupwork versus curriculum. Project workers also need to guard against abusing and consequently losing the trust they develop with young people by unconsciously becoming 'agents of control' for the school.

If a youth social work project is to make effective choices about its work and priorities, the staff must know their 'patch', where young people live, congregate and socialise. They must have an awareness of the environment inhabited by the young people and the pressures and influences they are subject to. Services must be offered with sensitivity, understanding and acceptance. They must also be familiar with the local statutory network, not just agency hierarchies but the attitudes and policies that have shaped and developed existing services. They need the ability to work with their colleagues in schools, and on occasions, the confidence and the tact to disagree with them.

(My thanks to colleagues Fraser Parkinson and Jane Kelly for contributing examples of their work.)

Chapter 9

Residential Schools After List 'D'

Andrew McCracken

In 1860, James Watt of Milne Square, Edinburgh, a boy of 11 with no previous convictions, was sentenced to 14 days' imprisonment and five years' detention in a reformatory school for stealing a bottle of hair oil from a barrow. The establishment of reformatory and industrial schools was the Victorian response to the 'perishing' and 'dangerous' children whose conditions and behaviour in overcrowded and insanitary cities was described by Chadwick and Dickens and prompted the efforts of such celebrated philanthropists as Mary Carpenter, Dr Guthrie and Sheriff Watson. Many of today's residential schools in Scotland can trace their origins to the reformatories, and many of the issues still being discussed, both about management and about ethos, have their origins in the mid 19th century: welfare or justice, care or control, sinner or sinned against, treatment or punishment, integration or segregation.

Reformatory schools were voluntarily managed but had legal powers to detain children and were subject to government inspection. Nevertheless, life for James Watt and his many successors was tough and unforgiving. Children in both reformatory and industrial schools underwent 'a disciplined and oppressive routine of hard work, severe punishment, austere living conditions, and a spartan diet' to attempt to eradicate the alleged 'defects of their characters, the evil influence of their previous environment, and the sins of their fathers' (Hurt 1988). The industrial training provided by the schools was generally poor, and on their discharge most children entered unskilled occupations or the armed forces. The distinction between the two types of school was administratively abolished in 1932 when both became approved schools, that is approved by the Secretary of State to accept children sentenced by the courts.

The Kilbrandon Committee took the view that the distinction between the potential and the actual offender was an arbitrary and artificial one, and concluded that both groups had suffered the same failures of upbringing and had the same need for special educational measures (1964). The subsequent Social Work (Scotland) Act 1968 anticipated that the approved schools would be part and parcel of the reconstruction in which the local authority social work departments would become responsible for the provision of comprehensive and flexible services responsive and relevant to local community need. It was determined that the schools should continue to be registered with the Secretary of State until decisions on their future could be made. The temporary title List 'D' was the result of the schools being on the fourth of a sequence of lists kept by the Scottish Education Department, and the intention was that they should be known by their name rather than their administrative category.

Regimes which had continued the very authoritarian and penal attitudes to children in trouble of their founders and which depended to a large extent on restriction of liberty as a means of control were forced to seek new ways of working with their charges as power passed from the managers of the institution to the new social work departments and children's panels. The response of the schools to the challenge presented to them by the rapidly changing attitudes of the emerging social work profession and the public was described as empirical and tentative and varied from school to school (SED-SWSG 1983). If the title List 'D' suggested that the schools were broadly similar, in practice there were considerable differences in regime, differences which reflected the different locations, sizes, facilities and staff groups of the schools. There were, however, two common points of reference. The first was that, with the exception of two schools in Strathclyde, the schools were voluntarily managed, nearly half of them by the churches. The second was that almost all of the children were compulsorily required to reside there as a result of a decision by a children's panel. The schools, not matter how liberal their regime, were still the main means of residential disposal by the panel for adolescents who had offended or were deemed beyond parental control.

The decade and a half during which the List 'D' schools remained under voluntary ownership and management with Scottish Education Department administration and funding was characterised by an open and sometimes acrimonious debate about future management arrangements and a less public or publicised discussion about the role of the schools in relation to other local resources for children. These discussions took place against the background of a decrease in demand for residential school places caused in part by demographic factors and in part by increasing willingness on the part of placing authorities to develop and use alternative community resources such as intermediate treatment or community carers, as well as increasing use of children's homes for children subject to compulsory supervision. In 1979 there were 26 List 'D' schools dealing with over 1,500 children. By April 1986, when central government finally withdrew from the administration and financing of all but the secure units, there were only 14 schools, including three with secure units, accommodating around 850 children in all (Toman 1986). The withdrawal of central government administration left the schools nameless in both senses of the term. The Fiddes Report of 1983 had criticised educational standards at the schools as 'abysmally low', and in April 1986 List 'D'; was closed. For a time the schools were referred to as former List 'D' schools, but are now generally known as residential schools for children with social, emotional and behavioural difficulties, or simply residential schools.

The withdrawal of central government involvement with the schools put to an end any lingering notion of a national system of residential schooling and propelled the schools and the local authority users into dialogue about the role of the schools within their local network of child care and educational resources. Some entered into user agreements with local authorities who took over their funding with the assistance of an increase in their rate support grant from central government. In one region, the two remaining schools were taken over by the local authority and managed through the Social Work Department. Some of the schools which had closed reopened under private ownership and management, and continued to work with broadly the same category of pupils. In some cases, they reopened as List 'G' schools, registered with the Scottish Education Department and taking pupils with special educational needs. The present mixed economy in terms of ownership, management and registration is mirrored by considerable geographical variations in both types and numbers of schools. Some regions have excess provision, others are unable to meet the demand for places and have to send children long distances to receive residential education. The recent HMI Report 'Choosing with Care' noted that there were considerable local differences in the way pupils with social, emotional and behavioural difficulties were dealt with. Pupils of comparable age and background with similar problems could be treated quite differently depending upon where they happened to live, due largely to inconsistencies in the range, type and quality of support on offer (SED 1990).

The context in which the discussions between schools and local authorities have taken place has been one in which there has been an increase in the emphasis on accountability in the public services. Local authorities have come under pressure from central government to control expenditure and to ensure they obtain value for money in the services they run or fund. A consequence of this is the questioning of the effectiveness of residential care and education as a strategy for intervening positively with children and families. Approaches have been favoured which direct resources at supporting vulnerable people in the community and reducing the dependence on Victorian institutions. The terms 'normalisation', 'mainstreaming' and 'integration' overlap considerably but each refer to the process of ending the exclusion of particular groups from facilities available to the rest of the community. In relation to children with social, emotional and behavioural difficulties, this means dealing with their problems wherever possible by keeping them in their local community and using the resources of the family and other local resources in a flexible manner. This indeed is the guiding principle of a number of regional youth strategies aimed at diverting resources away from the provision of alternative education and care and towards the child's own school and family. a corollary of this principle is that children should be provided with care and education in the least restrictive environment possible for them to achieve social, emotional and academic growth and development.

The operation of policies which promote integration should ensure that only those youngsters who cannot cope or be coped with in less supported or structured environments find their way into residential schools. It should also ensure that those who can return to a more 'ordinary' environment after a period in residential school are enabled to do so. This may have a number of consequences on the residential schools. Placement in residential education may come to be seen as a mark of failure rather than a positive choice, the last resort rather than a strategy for intervention. Schools which are unable to respond to the challenge presented by increasing integration, due to their location, their facilities or their regime may no longer be viable, and some may close.

There is certainly evidence of an increase in the degree of concentration of difficult children in residential care which has had its effects on stability and standards of care in many children's homes. It is not that the children's behaviour is necessarily any more difficult than it was. It is rather that the threshold for admission to residential care has risen with the development of diversionary strategies resulting in a child in care population which is different from the one the buildings and staff ratios were designed for, with many youngsters who have a history of failure in previous placements and a self-image which reflects these damaging experiences. Children may have missed months, or even years, of schooling through truancy or exclusion before their eventual admission to residential school.

Wherever they are situated the schools, then, are generally fulfilling a similar role and function in relation to other regional resources for children, in that they provide a last chance of working constructively with difficult and damaged children in less intrusive facilities, just as the secure units fulfil the same role for the schools. There are, still, however, considerable differences between the schools in terms of how they fulfil this role. At least one school has deliberately geared its service to the post 16 year old. a small proportion have become co-educational whilst others remain single sex, mainly boys. Some provide 7 day a week care, others are predominantly weekly boarding. Most of the schools have set up a day attendance facility, some to a far greater extent than others, depending mainly on their location in relation to centres of population.

This depends on a fundamental recasting of the relationship between parent and professional. Whilst the reformatories and approved schools provided, to a large extent, a substitute for families which were deemed inadequate to the task of parenting, the List 'D' schools moved increasingly towards working with

Chapter 9

families and using their resources to support children and families in more innovative and imaginative ways. Some schools used formal groupwork approaches with families, others worked on an individual casework basis. As schools became increasingly associated with their local community, day attendance became possible for some pupils. The realisation that many children could remain at home and benefit from the education provision at the schools without disrupting their residential regime has led, in many cases, to schools being prepared to draw up flexible packages of care and education to suit the needs of the individual and his or her circumstances. Within the same establishment this may vary from full 7 day a week care and education for up to 52 weeks per year through a range of shared care (and sometimes education) packages with families or substitute carers, to respite or short term care. There is often the facility to adjust the package to suit changing family or individual circumstances. For the most part, residential care is short-term, and links with the family or alternative carers can be actively encouraged and developed.

Recent years have also seen major changes in the education provision at the schools, which have been concerned with providing a curriculum which is closer to the 'mainstream'. Stung by the criticism contained in the Fiddes report, and taking advantage of several new initiatives in secondary and further education, many of the schools developed Standard Grade, National Certificate and SEB short Course work. At their best, the schools can offer a level of personalised support which assists pupils to attain targets they could not hope to achieve in mainstream schools. In some cases, schools are included in the Technical and Vocational Initiative (TVEI) arrangements with their local education authority. Residential schools are increasingly able to offer parents and pupils to exercise a series of choices in the curriculum, between a modified and supported mainstream academic curriculum and a more vocationally based one; between certification through Standard Grade and through SCOTVEC; and between returning to mainstream school and completing statutory schooling in the residential school. Some schools are involved in in-service training with mainstream colleagues on a neighbourhood or regional basis, or through TVEI or headteacher training. an increasing number of pupils have access to the experiences offered to ordinary school pupils such as, for example, education/industry links, college visits and tasters and access to outdoor centres. Some schools have developed links with local secondary schools and pupils are able to attend on a full or part-time basis.

It is hard to disagree with those who argue that no placement in residential education can be justified on purely educational grounds. For most pupils in residential education, school difficulties are one of a number of interrelated features which precipitate admission. Not everyone would go as far as Booth who argues that 'the only legitimate arguments [for segregated education] are those for isolation; that there is a group of pupils who need to be isolated from the mainstream either because this is a precondition for their education or because it is necessary for their protection or for the protection of others' (O.U.). Segregated education can, at its worst, further educationally disadvantage children who are often socially and emotionally disadvantaged, but at best it can prepare pupils to take advantage of mainstream opportunities in the broadest sense, whether they leave the school to return to mainstream or at the conclusion of their statutory education.

Summary and Conclusion

The withdrawal of the Scottish Education Department from the administration and financing of the List 'D' schools was laughingly compared to the double decker bus from which the driver and conductor decided to get off, leaving the passengers to their own devices. David Colvin, the then chief adviser to the Social Work Services Group explained to the Reporters' Conference in 1985 that one of the reasons they got off the bus was that all the passengers were in dispute about where they wanted to go in the first place, and as some of the passengers actually owned the bus, the driver and the conductor were in an impossible position.

There would appear to be no longer any meaningful distinction between the different categories of List 'D' and List 'G' schools. There is instead a range of approaches being practised, from schools which offer secure conditions within which care and education are carried out, to the therapeutic schools which offer a more radical alternative community living experience. The former List 'D' schools occupy a broad middle ground along with, and no longer distinguishable from, a number of the List 'G' schools.

The recent scandals which have affected residential care and education may result in increased vetting of staff, and in more stringent standards in registration and inspection of schools. It is expected that significantly greater resources will be devoted to training and developing staff at all levels, and that staffing ratios will be examined and improved. Yet there is a notable lack of empirical research in to models of good practice in the delivery and management of residential care and education, and, crucially, into the effectiveness of the various forms of intervention now available. This is perhaps not surprising as performance indicators are difficult to determine in relation to the care and education of children with social, emotional and behavioural difficulties and tend to concentrate on what is easy to quantify. Further research could usefully illuminate this area, and establish whether any benefits derived from residential education can be sustained when the pupil moves away from the supports available within the residential setting.

The deregistration of the List 'D' schools accelerated the process which should have happened in 1971, namely the development towards an integrated child care and education service on a regional basis, with the schools playing their part in the range of provision for children with social, emotional and behavioural difficulties. Inevitably that role will have a strong residual element in it due to the potentially extremely intrusive nature of the intervention. But the development of a range of services based round a central core of residence allows the schools which are working with a local population to be more flexible and imaginative in developing programmes of care and education which are matched to the individual's needs and circumstances and which offer each the least restrictive intervention consistent with continued social, emotional and educational development.

References

Booth, T. *Learning for All.* Open University, E241 Unit 1/2

Colvin, D (1985). *Draft Speech to Reporters Conference.*

Hurt, J S (1988). *Outside the Mainstream.*

Kilbrandon Report (1964). *Children and Young Persons Scotland.*

SED (1990). *Choosing with Care.*

SED Social Work Services Group (1983). *Future of List 'D' Schools (The Fiddes Report).*

Toman, M (1986). *Residential Special Education in Scotland for Children with Emotional, Social and Behavioural Difficulties.* Scottish Education Review Information Paper 17.

Chapter 10

Moving Towards Change: The Role of People, Place and Programme in Creating a Residential Therapeutic Environment for Children

David Dean

(This chapter originated as a paper first delivered in Moscow in October 1990 to a meeting of 50 Directors of Special Schools and their associated psychotherapists.)

What more difficult a situation could a family in crisis be asked to face than to commit itself to agreeing to one of its children leaving home for a residential school or community. For despite the gravity of the problems which will have brought them to this point in their lives, the agony of the impending separation is considerable. The family finds itself caught between two painful extremes. One the one hand, they are both the perpetrators and the victims of their family's disintegrating wholeness, a process which has weakened and alarmed them, and on the other hand they experience a serious loss in self-esteem and control over their affairs which can render them emotionally traumatised.

The children of these families are, however, the more fortunate of all the children with whom we work. The family I have described suggests a mother, a father and a number of children. My picture also suggests that, despite the damage they are suffering, there is the potential for investment or re-investment amongst themselves. When a child in these circumstances enters our school/community, there must be two essential questions which are asked.

1. How do we support this family and allow the child frequent enough access to it so that whatever success he or she may have within our community can be regularly carried home and seen within that context?

2. Can we look ahead and make at least the first guess as to when, if at all, this child should return to mainstream day schooling and eventually to home?

There are other children, however, whose circumstances make it inappropriate for us to be thinking in these terms at all. For these children the 'investment' from the family or the parenting figures is either absent through negligence on the part of the adults or it has become polluted and twisted in bizarre fashion resulting in the child holding only a frightening and grossly inadequate concept of what families are all about.

George

George's mother came from a small village in the Scottish Highlands where secrets in the family are held onto very tightly. Only the people who had been in the village for several generations knew of George's family affairs. All newcomers who had arrived in the last twenty years or so were excluded from any gossip or discussion.

George's mother had several brothers and sisters. The identity of George's father was a close secret and never spoken about. One night, on a fast, wet road, following a bout of drinking alcohol, the car in which George's mother was travelling, with a new boyfriend, left the road and crashed. George's mother was killed instantly. George was three years old and was staying that night at the house of his mother's parents in the same village.

In the family discussions which followed, the grandparents decided they would look after the young boy. At the age of five, he started school and there were immediate difficulties. When he was seven years old, his grandmother died and, within two months, his grandfather married the woman in the next door house and moved in with her, disposing of his own house. This lady did not like George and so he went to live with his mother's eldest sister, again in the same village. There were still problems at school; George interfered with other children, both in their work and at play, he was aggressive and threatening and was frequently violent. The elder sister of his mother had children of her own and she and her husband liked to be able to leave the children at nights with a childminder and go out.

George, however, could not be left and so it was decided that in future he would be shared amongst the four families of his late mother's brothers and sisters. He had a plastic bag with his few possessions and from the age of eight would go to whichever house he was directed to for the night. In one of these houses, at the age of nine, he was sexually abused and penetrated by a male childminder. This fact was not known until he was twelve years old and resident with us. Between the time he was living with his extended family and his arrival with us, he had lived in three children's homes, two foster homes and had had five changes of school.

By the time he arrived at Raddery, he had experienced eleven changes of home, eleven or more patterns of parenting, fifteen rejections and fifteen messages telling him that he frightened other people, children and adults alike, by his awesome power. He became fascinated, yet distressed, by this power; it was a power disproportionate in every sense an one which made other people move away from his or give him messages that he was bad. Some even thought him mad.

Chapter 10

The truth was that, although he could appear as both of these, he was in fact extremely, extremely, sad.

It is to this child's world of disproportionate power, his own fear of his impact on those around him, his lack of any mother bonding and his stifled and misunderstood self-expression and creativity that we were asked to bring our skills and our commitment. We learn in our work that each time a young child suffers yet another change of home base, his likelihood of gaining stability, as an integrated person, is substantially reduced.

And not only to George but also to Katherine and Anne whose behaviour was rooted in their brain disfunction and inappropriate handling at school and home; to Robert who lived with his large family until the day when, at seven years old, he discovered he was related to none of them, except his mother; to Fiona who was ritually tied up and beaten by a perverse and inadequate father. To these children and all their counterparts the therapeutic intervention of a skilled group working in a residential environment which gives an unequivocal message of being safe is perhaps the only possible way forward. It needs a programme which addresses their psychological and spiritual needs and one in which their intellectual and creative potential can emerge and be nurtured.

I have chosen to use the titles of People, Place and Programme as categories which are useful in looking at the work of a school/community for emotionally damaged children.

You will note that in my paper, I use terms like 'psychologically disfunctioning', 'maladjusted' and 'emotionally damaged'. I am not, you will see, concentrating on the issue of delinquency alone. For many of our children, delinquency is not a problem in isolation. It is the manifestation of much deeper pathological damage which it is our task to confront. Of course there are children whose acting out of their pathological state has brought them to the heights of law breaking and so entrenched are they in this way of behaving that they are not reachable in schools or communities like ours. This situation, however, is not common.

I would like to say something of the three categories I have referred to.

People

I do not subscribe to the notion that quite ordinary and moderately competent workers can be recruited to work in our schools and that, in order that they may survive the pressures involved, a whole system of limiting safeguards has to be devised for their safety. This results in a mediocre organisation and programme which does little to engage the children at the level at which they are functioning and transport them on to the wavelength necessary for the process of healing and growth to take place. Neither am I recommending outrageous leadership from adults but I would, at all costs, avoid having faceless and bureaucratic workers in direct contact with children. Staff members, who need to be dragged unwillingly into contact with the fantasy world our children inhabit, or whose sense of adventure is so impaired that they cannot connect with the natural, let alone the unnatural surges of adolescence, or whose need for a personal security is so tightly held that they cannot approach a relationship with the unloved and potentially unlovable - these workers are not best suited to our kind of work.

When I was in the Leningrad Special School in May, I was invited to see several formal classes in progress. The one I liked the best had the teacher, a lady who was by no means young herself, easily and naturally conversing with a boy on details of Russian architecture in the city of Leningrad. She was using some film slides which she was showing to the class. In fact, I knew the boy better than I know the teacher. His name was Andrei and he had been a visitor to our school in Scotland last January.

What was impressive here was the teacher's skill in getting this boy to interact with her at the highest level possible for him. He was not a passive recipient of information; he was participating in his own education in a very real way. How vital it is to have staff members with these skills and how essential it is that in as many of the staff group as possible there is present the ability to connect not just at an intellectual level but at a social and psychological level too.

We can interact with a pupil in a discussion about architecture or mathematics, music or literature. Are we also prepared, by virtue of our own training and understanding, to engage with him on the issues to do with his own identity, his sexuality and his family relationships? Furthermore, can a health number of staff members manage a small group of such children together so that, as well as having their own individual session with a competent, they can also join with other children with parallel experiences of deprivation and confusion and gain new insight from the security and wealth of exchange in the group? Can the staff members respond to an ongoing staff development and support programme and will enough time be devoted to it in any one year?

We have found it useful to develop such a programme for which we allow fourteen full days a year. Five of these days are in August, before any children return from their summer holidays. This block of five days we call Community Week and during this time we organise in detail our individual treatment for each child and we look at the overall educational and therapeutic programme. We might examine essentials of primary care, such as feeding, toileting, sleeping and clothing. These are not seen just as organisational issues but as representing the very core of our children's emotional requirements.

If the neurotic, or almost neurotic, feeling of danger a girl experiences through not having privacy in toileting is not recognised, then presumably institutions could continue for years in making minimum provision for its children's most basic needs, blissfully unaware of the perverse behaviours such provision is keeping alive and quite unprepared for making the most appropriate use of funds for refurbishment of such areas as bedrooms, bathrooms, kitchen and dining areas, when they become available.

Within the staff group there must always be enough understanding and knowledge to address these fundamental points. Consultants can advise, require action even, but for real progress to be made, the knowledge and the implementing of that knowledge has to be the property of the staff group. It properly belongs to them and, if they invest in its future, the outcome for the children will be all the better.

Other days of staff support and development are directed towards grasping knowledge new to us and for this we do need to hear from practitioners in other places. In these tasks, researchers, psychologists and psychiatrists all place their part. For the staff group to move as one, though, a level of contact and commitment to each other needs to be developed. Our community has always worked on the holistic principle of engaging every single person on the payroll in the therapeutic process. No one can justifiably say 'I teach at Raddery' or 'I cook at Raddery' or 'I houseparent at Raddery'. All members of the staff, with the exception of the secretaries, are engaged to work with children. Of course, we all have our specialisms and we appreciate each other's skills but in holistic working for the overall benefit of psychologically damaged children, we do not neglect to train the cook!

A part of this process requires us to develop a professional intimacy; to be able to interpret each other's non-verbal language, to recognise stress and to co-work to the highest standard imaginable. Therefore some games involving co-operation rather than competition, trust rather than deceit, are as important for the staff to play as they are for the children. We see it as essential that we build ourselves into a body of people who can provide security for the openly hostile, warmth for the fearful, understanding for the misunderstood and time and even more time for us all. We all know just how much we struggle to achieve these goals and we must be glad when we can even approach attaining them.

One final attribute in staff members, I would like to mention here, is a sense of vulnerability. If the message of security to the children's group has been successfully absorbed and there is an appropriate air of predictability in the establishment, still allowing for spontaneity and behavioural upset even, it must be a revelation for children who, in their families have seen largely the extremes of adult interaction, to witness the gentle teasing of one member of staff by another, shared humour, or a self-deprecating remark in front of the whole group from the director, who is secure enough in himself to make it. If we need to parade constantly our absolute competence in front of the children, are we not demonstrating a role model, not so far removed from the parenting models which took some of our children from their homes in the first place?

Place

What of the environment in which all this work takes place. You know how it is as a director. You have a little knowledge when you start, except that you do not see it quite like that at the time. I suspect that, at whatever level we thought our knowledge, qualifications and experience were, when we were appointed, ten years on and we realise that we were only just starting.

The knowledge we do have at the beginning serves us well, however, and it becomes either challenged or reinforced as we progress. In 1979, at the start of my school, I invited a colour therapist and designer to look at our buildings and to recommend to us a colour scheme which would contribute to the healing process. The Waldorf Schools founded throughout Europe on the principles of the nutritionist and teacher, Rudolph Steiner, knew much about the effect of colour and texture on children's sensory deprivations. The scheme was complicated and involved using a bonding colour, in this case a coral salmon pink, for all corridors. From there the scheme was sequential and a journey throughout the building would take us through the bonding, coral salmon pink colour, to greens and white to aid digestion to reds for invigoration in learning areas and to blues in layers for sleeping and passive areas. Five years later I met Melvyn Rose who was, as Founder Director of Peper Harow, several years ahead of us in our work. He told me about the work of the American psychologist and psychiatrist, the late Dr Bruno Bettleheim, founder of the Orthogenic School in Chicago, whose ideas about creating an appropriate environment for the treating of emotionally disturbed adolescents, I read with fascination. Not only was he reinforcing to the provision we had already made but he explained in psycho-therapeutic terms why our intuition was right to lead us in that direction. But I learned much more. We had not seen the deeper implications for children of our less than adequate privacy in toileting and bathing. The relevance of providing a recumbent mother figure in stone which invited and received all kinds of abuse as well as loving actions became clear.

It became only too clear to me last week, when I listened intently to the story of a young girl of nineteen years old, the daughter of one of my colleagues, who has just returned to Scotland from spending two months in an orphanage in Romania. There she endured the behaviour of children eight years old and upwards, naked in their rooms with negligible access to the green grass outside who, to prevent her leaving them after her allotted time, would not only rock to and fro moaning and banging their heads on the walls but would bite deeply at her ears and urinate on her chest. The regression which Bettleheim was allowing for by the provision of the recumbent mother figure in stone was identical to that which the Romanian orphans were exhibiting as their only known response to their being denied a mothering figure.

We had also taken into account quite early on the value of planned lighting, allowing for the softening of rooms when appropriate and the highlighting of features for their practical or symbolic significance. Our dining tables were oval in shape and made of inch thick Scots pine. They could be converted into seats with a high back and solid arms to place in front of a log fire. The plates, cups and saucers were of substantial hand-made earthenware pottery, painted in earth colours and made in the Highlands of Scotland. The cups were of such a shape as to give symbolic breast-like comfort to the child who grasped the warm bowl. Cutlery was also heavy-weight and does not yield easily to the tortuous twisting of anxious and destructive fingers.

Another thing we knew was that animals, carefully chosen and accommodated, could contribute significantly to some children's frail attempts to make relationships. Neither Dr Bettleheim nor anyone else could teach us much about the potential here; we were on our own. And as a result we have, in the last five years, acted as a source of reference for various interested communities both in Europe and in North America. True, we discovered one or two miniature zoos where children were allowed to look at the animals through wire fences with no involvement beyond that. There were other places which sported the school dog, poor beast, or had a solitary chained goat treading the same circle of bare earth painfully but displayed with such pride in order to say 'we keep animals!' What did children gain from this? Their teachers not only failed to understand the needs of the animals, but also failed in addressing the potential that animals hold for offering comfort for the child who is not yet ready to speak out, or for one who needs to make an investment in another creature, though perhaps not yet a human one. At a more natural and sophisticated level a child's genuine interest in the welfare of an animal or bird can grow to take precedence over her own needs. At this point the child is discovering just what making a sacrifice for another is all about. She is putting her needs aside for the time being. For the child who is ready to do this, it is a clear step forward.

I often watch with amazement as children whose relationship sustaining capabilities are negligible come into our animal area at 8.30 each morning and again at night to demonstrate amongst our goats, sheep, hens, ducks and geese just how well they can contain their natural inclination towards self-indulgence.

One year an inspired worker built a little house from old oak beams. It is sited in a field near to the main buildings of the school. To this structure, he added the old wheelhouse from a wooden ferryboat long since disused. Almost every child in our community must have been involved in the construction at one time. No machinery was used except for the crane which lifted the wheelhouse into place. The foundations were dug by hand and every wooden peg carefully made on site and hammered home. The wooden titles on the roof were in place before winter and glass, some of it coloured and in beautifully irregular shaped frames, put into the windows.

The Oakhouse, as it is called, was the product of fervour and joint effort. It was to be our centre for magic and treats. Shortly after it was finished, three boys were allowed to sleep the night there. Two of them took cigarettes with them and one persuaded another to commit a sexually indecent act. It seemed that the Oakhouse could not be quite theirs until they had acted perversely in it.

Fortunately, the resultant Community Meeting looked at the issue constructively. Whilst many people felt strongly about their creation being used in this way, others divorced the act between the two boys from their feelings for the Oakhouse. After about an hour's intensive discussion, we were drawn to acknowledge the impropriety of the boys' action and to rededicate the Oakhouse as a centre for magic and treats. It has since become a haven for the children who love to play at being captain on the bridge, space rocket pilot, Robinson Crusoe on a desert island or defenders of the castle. Its very flexibility and its unreality is what make it so solid and so real.

We have one room in each we meet each day, not to discuss business or to examine group behaviour but to bond with each other. It is this room which we call the Meeting House and upon which the Raddery Room at the Leningrad Special School is modelled. The Meeting House has been described by a visiting writer on maladjusted children to Raddery as 'the symbolic hand of the healing process' which he discovered there. Here stories are told, legends re-enacted. We make music and sing without a fraction of the usual embarrassment teenagers suffer in this. Books are read and trust games played. Using the whole carpet in the middle of the Meeting House and round which we sit on low chairs, the leader of a recent meeting enacted the story of the last expedition of the explorer Captain Scott to the wastes of antarctica. The whole carpet represented antarctica itself. Scott reached the South Pole in the middle of the carpet several weeks after the Norwegian Amundsen who travelled from the opposite direction represented by one edge of the carpet. Sickness, insufficiency of food and the severity of the weather made the journey back slow and exhausting. Two of the five man party died on the way and the remaining three men, including Captain Scott, died on or around March 27, 1912. In November that year, a search party found Captain Scott's tent, his records and diaries just five miles from their base at another edge of the carpet. In his final letter to his wife, Scott had said in respect of his infant son, who was born while he was away, 'make the boy fond of nature, it is better than games'. That boy grew to be one of the first men to recognise the importance of protecting the planet and devoted much of his life to the cause with considerable effect. The children in the Meeting House look wistful. Their emotions are moved for the leader is expert at engaging with young people at this level. Furthermore, they hear that they are invited to tour Captain Scott's ship, the Discovery, now she has returned to the Scottish city in which she was built. Plans are soon to be made.

There is the customary reflective silence at the end of the meeting and then a haunting Scottish song about the return of this ship to its native port after many years absence is played. We leave the Meeting House to commence the rest of the day's lessons and activities.

So much has already been said about the Programme in the two sections I have just covered People and Place. Suffice to say here, that our Programme reflects each child's need for three kinds of time:

1. structured time
2. semi-structured time
3. unstructured time

Before we can assume a child will manage beyond Raddery with any real success, they must be able to cope with each category of time. It would be too simple for us to occupy every available hour of the child's day in tightly structured activity. Many children will need this for quite some time but, as they progress, they will require to develop coping strategies for the future when not everything is organised for them. Their subject learning in English, Mathematics, Science, Social Skills, Art and Music needs to carry an element of private study, just as soon as it is likely to succeed.

Responsibilities which each boy and girl has in the Community are, by tradition, carried out when staffing numbers are fairly low. Logs are chopped for the wood stoves, the kitchen is cleared of the breakfast things, bells are polished and goats milked. The Meeting House is prepared for the Morning Meeting and the visitors' waiting room got ready. Older children from our Half-way House in the town arrive by minibus for their meeting with me. An old ship's bell rings and we walk together to the Meeting House.

Expeditions in mountain country should carry an element of acceptable risk if they are to have any of the value they do hold for more stable young people. In structured time we must continue to make demands too. We must tackle intellectual needs by a thorough education programme with external certification where appropriate and group work should address emotional issues. The whole day, including all its component parts, from rise to bed, is the therapeutic process. There are no exclusions and everyone is involved. More and more contact outside the community becomes possible.

Some of our older pupils will be working in the community for experience. Graham is going to the hotel to work in the kitchen. Lechlan will go to the pottery and today is working on the making of jugs. Margaret has had her first successful two days with a ladies' hairdresser. Finlay is helping to make a gate at the blacksmith's. Gavin and Tracey worked behind the stage one day a week for three months at the theatre in the big town. They are all preparing to leave us. John is staying with us at our Half-way House until he is seventeen. He will attend the local day school to sit for his Higher examinations.

The Annual Gathering of Families in September has three children out of forty unrepresented. 'Why won't my parents come?' moans Gary but we knew they would not be there and made special arrangements for him. Nothing, however, can quite compensate Gary for their absence. The drama performance, the music, the parents' meeting with the staff and me, and the visits to class teachers and group leaders go really well and the staff detect a greater level of interest and good questioning from the parents. Even this festival weekend, though, does not rival the value of the small area parents' groups which meet in the house of one family in the area from time to time. In these meetings eight parents can keep two or three staff members actively discussing the issues common to them all for several hours - how to handle the children during periods at home, prospects for what happens after Raddery, learning to understand their own feelings as parents; feelings of guilt and reaching for clues right back to their childhood and resurrecting painful memories of how they themselves were parented. 'Take on the child and we take on the family' has been our measure if at all possible; and of course sometimes it is not possible and we must not pretend to the child or to ourselves that it is otherwise.

Conclusion

The possibilities of therapeutic intervention with a community of children and adults living and working together are exciting but it is always a high risk business. A new culture for the group and new perspectives for the individual are attainable by careful selection of the staff for their understanding and therapeutic potential as workers.

The environment in which this work takes place must reflect the philosophy of giving security, allowing for fantasy and exploring creativity to encourage each child to move towards achieving their potential.

The Programme needs to be flexible enough to accommodate both the unintegrated child who is struggling to make even the first relationship in his life and whose capacity to respond adequately in groups is minimal, to the integrated young person whose eyes are now looking beyond the intensity and special nature of this community to the next period in his life when the support systems which

Chapter 10

have sustained him, for several years, in his endeavours to move beyond his disturbed state are removed.

However many children can be rescued by programmes which allow them to remain at home and in their day schools, there will always be a small proportion of any nation's children for whom the only responsible action is to immerse them in a radical alternative to their current life style which is at the root of their disfunctioning and their distress. This is the work in which we are privileged to be engaged. Raising our levels of awareness for the future wellbeing of our children is a task for all of us and it is a task which offers ever new horizons.

Chapter 11

Education in a Psychiatric Setting

Deirdre Leach

For a minority of children a short spell of residential treatment in a psychiatric unit enables assessment and treatment to be given with the necessary intensity and immediacy.

In Lothian the in-patient unit of the Department of Child and Family Psychiatry is Forteviot. The average length of admissions is four months. Weekends spent at home and daily contact with family through visits, family therapy sessions and phone calls ensure that the child's place is kept for him and that problems continue to be seen within the context of the family even after admission. Referrals are made initially to the out-patient department mainly by general practitioners and the Royal Hospital for Sick Children but they also come from the Departments of Social Work and Education Psychology. On average 800 new referrals are seen at DCFP in a year. Of these only an average of 35 children are admitted to Forteviot.

The decision to remove a child from him home and his school for a period of in-patient assessment and treatment is not one that is ever taken lightly.

Reasons for admission

Often the reason for admission is likely to be that home - or clinic - based treatment has not proved sufficient. It is sometimes impossible to make an accurate assessment when a family is seen at fortnightly intervals for one hour sessions. Or it may be that no change has been effected by the various interventions and the reason for this failure has not become clear. Intensive observation of the child in the different settings within the in-patient unit is therefore necessary.

Sometimes it is obvious that a child will not have his needs met effectively nor will his family be able to survive *except* through a brief and positive experience of separation and treatment of the child in a residential setting (Wells 1991). This gives both child and family a badly needed period of respite and time to offer family therapy in the hope of restoring the family in   tact. It takes the pressure off the child and gives him a chance to recover some of his self-esteem which will have been eroded by feelings of blame, shame, failure and guilt.

The classroom is no place for any form of intensive individual therapy which might leave the child feeling fragile and vulnerable to his peers.

Children benefit from opportunities to express themselves through music, art and drama as well as through creative writing in school. Children have few words for emotions and therefore are limited in their ability to conceptualize situations. By developing their vocabulary and providing experience through role-play and social skills games, children are helped to think in terms of a continuum of feelings and to understand variability in mood not only in themselves but hopefully in others. (Leach 1990)

Training

In order to maintain a therapeutic milieu a well-integrated consistently applied programme is needed.

To this end many opportunities are made available to all staff to attend workshops and lectures and an in-service training programme covers theory and practice of, for example, the various forms of therapy. *Ad hoc* lectures are set up at short notice to deal with any topic causing concern in the unit such as anorexia nervosa, sexual abuse, epilepsy.

In a multidisciplinary setting roles overlap considerably although each discipline contributes its own particular skills and retains its own identity. Shared training addresses the need for a consistent approach throughout the unit and helps to combat splitting and manipulation of staff by children. It also serves to keep staff interested and informed which in turn motivates. Due to the training needs of psychiatric staff the whole unit benefits from up-to-date information on research and new ideas.-

The way forward

In the seventies emphasis began to shift away from the search for problems, pathology and negative factors in the patient and family and to move towards identifying assets and positive attributes with which to work (Wardie 1991).

The 1990s are bringing more community-based work, promoting resilience in the child and protective factors in school and in society. More preventive work in schools and children's centres in the form of social skills groups or parents' management training groups would be beneficial as would an increase in teachers' in-service training focussing on issues of emotional, behavioural and psychological disturbance.

The Nuffield Child Psychology and Psychiatry Unit in collaboration with the Department of Education of the University of Newcastle-Upon-Tyne run a joint course for nurses and teachers. Interdisciplinary training using established programmes in psychiatric units is not only an efficient deployment of resources but advantageous in that the focus is wider than it would be for a specific profession.

Social work and education services are now working more closely together in most areas of Scotland. It is to be hoped that this decade will signal the coming together of clinicians and educationalists. If the concept of the 'whole' child in the context of his home, school and community is to be meaningful this would seem to be the best way forward.

Concerted effort is needed by all disciplines and agencies to understand each other's differences and work together. Differences of approach and practice can be viewed positively and can lead to healthy evolution as long as opinions are not held with delusional fervour.

Wardle (1991) tabulates some of the more exaggerated splits in child psychiatry. He entitles the table 'Maleficent Dichotomies' because of the harm they have done in depriving children of balanced care and child rearing. Wardle suggests that if 'versus' is removed from the table we are left with a list of concepts and strategies comprising a comprehensive service for children. None need be in opposition or worse still, competition!

Methods/Ideas	*Counter-Methods/Counter Ideas*
Nature	Nurture
Behaviourism	Psychoanalysis
Psychological methods	Medical methods
Child guidance	Hospital child psychiatry
Residential treatment	Community treatment
Family therapy	Individual therapy
Control & discipline	Loving nurture
Professional autonomy	Team work
Confidentiality	Open communication
Audit & good management	Professional freedoms
Measurement & scientific methods	Descriptive humanitarian methods
Belief in standards	Tolerance of deviance
Educational methods	Therapeutic method

McKay (1987) identifies a lack of evidence to suggest that the teaching within psychiatric wards or residential schools does provide special or effective teaching. Howlin (1985) states: 'Vague and untested notions of providing social therapy abound and education is often neglected'.

Chapter 11

There is obviously a need for research into the area of educational provision in psychiatric units throughout Britain not only to allay such generalised misconceptions but also to identify and build on existing good practice.

References

Barker, P (1974). *The Residential Psychiatric Treatment of Children.* Crosby Lockwood Staple. London.

Barker, P (1986). *Basic Child Psychiatry, 4th Edition.* Collins.

Howlin, P (1985). Special educational treatment. In Rutter, M and Hersov, L (eds) *Child and Adolescent Psychiatry: Modern Approaches, 2nd Edition.* Blackwell. London.

Leach, D (1990). Teaching in a psychiatric unit. In Bovair, K and Baker, D (eds) *Making the the Special Schools Ordinary? Volume 2.* The Falmer Press.

McKay, R (1987). Educational provision in residential psychiatric units. SED final report: *Educational Psychologists' Professional Development Initiative.*

Rutter, M, Tizard, J and Whitmore, K (1970). *Education, Health and Behaviour.* Longman.

Wardle, C J (1991). Twentieth century influences on the development in Britain of services for child and adolescent psychiatry. *British Journal of Psychiatry 159.* Pp 53-68.

Wells, P (1992). Survival in a cold climate. *Psychiatric Bulletin 16.* Pp 10-14.

Wolff, S (1971). *Children Under Stress.* Penguin.

Chapter 12

Secure Provision

Bill Duffy

As you read this chapter a small group of boys and girls, about eighty in number, will be receiving their care and education behind locked doors and barred windows within secure provision in the Child Care system in Scotland. Appropriately there is much concern expressed about the uses to which secure accommodation is put, the kinds of children being admitted and the quality of their life-style and education while detained. Secure units were initially established to manage absconding and violent, disruptive behaviour of a small minority of young people already subject to compulsory measures of care in the Child Care system. In the last thirty years there has been a proliferation of secure accommodation accompanied by a plethora of legislation and literature to appropriately manage and control this system, and to illuminate discussion on the efficacy of such drastic intervention in young peoples lives. It would be wrong to assume that, like Topsy in Uncle Tom's Cabin, secure provision has just 'growed', but within child care residential establishments in Britain it has certainly been an area of growth.

It would be safe for readers to assume that many, if not all of the 250 young people admitted annually to secure care in Scotland are perceived by referring agencies to exhibit extremes in both disruptive and/or disturbing behaviour, they are clearly perceived as the most troubled and troublesome young people in society. Young people admitted to secure care are drawn from the normal population and are submitted to similar pressures and experiences as their peers. Young people to-day more than ever appear to be targeted by media and advertising and as a result have significantly higher expectations and are driven by ever increasing 'wants' than previous generations. Family breakdowns through parental conflict, separation, divorce and even homelessness affect significant numbers of young people. Drug and alcohol abuse with resulting concerns for health and safety are a major concern. Sexual abuse, both as victims and perpetrators, are widely reported as being on the increase. Educational failure, truancy, expulsion and suspension are widely reported along with a mood of failure and depression about school amongst young people despite a decade of unprecedented curriculum reform. Teenage sex and fears about the spread of HIV infection in the young heterosexual population are a growing concern. Teenage pregnancies and abortions are increasing. Rates of offending by teenagers are increasing; violence amongst teenagers appears to be increasing; the catalogue of problems besetting youth to-day appears endless. Young people admitted to secure care have often experienced many of the diverse and multi-faceted difficulties outlined above, but perhaps more significantly for their admission to security they often have a history of running away from their problems and the agencies who attempt to intervene and engage them in tackling their difficulties. An escalation of their difficulties, linked via running away from home and/or absconding from care, leads to a significant deterioration in their conditions and their resultant marginalisation which propels society to even more severe forms of intervention, to the extent they are eventually locked up.

The first secure unit within the Child Care system in Britain was opened at Rossie near Montrose in 1962. During the ensuing three decades we have shown an increasing tendency as a society to lock up young people. In 1970 there were 1700 residential school places, in the then List D system, to deal with young people who required compulsory measures of care and education, of which only the 18 places at Rossie were within secure conditions. By comparison, in 1990 there were 700 residential school places available of which 80 were within secure conditions.

The present day map of secure child care in Scotland shows 3 large secure units each of 24 beds, and 4 smaller units ranging from 2 to 5 places. The three large secure units are located at Rossie, Kerelaw in Stevenson and St Mary's Kenmure in Bishopbriggs. Kerelaw is owned and managed by Strathclyde Region, and Rossie and St Mary's are voluntary agencies. The three large secure units were originally developed as units on large residential school campuses, but at St Mary's and Rossie only small residual non-secure facilities remain as a result of the closure by Central Government of their open school facilities. The four smaller secure units located in local authority residential establishments throughout Scotland are Howdenhall, Edinburgh with 5 places, the Polmont Youth Care Centre in Central Region with 2 places, Rimbleton House Young Persons Centre in Fife with 2 places, and Closeburn in Dumfries also with 2 places.

As a result of the Secure Accommodation [Scotland] Regulations 1983, the Secretary of State for Scotland has the responsibility to approve the various types of secure accommodation. Approval is granted and the units are registered by the Secretary of State for periods of three years, but only after inspection by Social Work Services Group and Her Majesty's Inspectors of Schools. Heads and Managers of secure accommodation in Scotland are also subject to a 'Code of Practice on the Use of Secure Accommodation for Children' issued on behalf of the Secretary of State in April 1985.

The function of the two types of secure accommodation as outlined in detail by the Code of Practice are distinctly different. At its simplest the three large secure units are intended for young people, of both sexes, who may need to be detained for some weeks, months, or in some instances years, as part of a programme of care and education. The smaller units are designed to function more often on an emergency basis, for young people who may require to be detained for only a smaller of hours or at the most, days. A number of smaller units are only staffed when in use and draw staffing resources from their main establishment, the large secure units on the other hand employ large groups of staff, sixty or more staff incorporating full-time educational staff as well as care and social work staff.

Legislation known as The Health and Social Security and Social Services Adjudication Act 1983 [HASSASSA] was enacted by Parliament to bring the Social Work [Scotland] At 1968 into line with Article 5:4 of the European Convention on Human Rights and to introduce a legally binding criteria which must be established before a young person can be detained in a child care secure unit. The law in Scotland requires that a young person detained in secure provision must have:

a) A history of absconding and
    i) he or she is likely to abscond unless kept in secure accommodation, and
    ii) if he or she absconds it is likely their physical, moral or mental welfare will be at risk or

b) he or she is likely to injure themselves or other persons unless kept in secure accommodation.

The European Convention on Human Rights requires 'Everyone who is deprived of his liberty on arrest or detention shall be entitled to take proceedings by which the lawfulness of his detention can be decided speedily by a court and his release ordered if the detention is not lawful'.

Young people in Scotland can be admitted to secure care by various routes which have distinct implications for the location of their placement and their length of stay. On an emergency basis the Director of Social Work and Head of a secure establishment can admit any young person, under the age of eighteen, by Administrative Process, if they are satisfied that the young person meets the criteria as established by HASSASSA. Their decision must be reviewed by a Children's Hearing or a court and the detention confirmed or terminated. A young person has the right to an expedited hearing within one working day of his or her admission. Young people are also admitted to secure care from Children's Hearings with an order naming the secure establishment and with an authorisation to utilise the secure unit. The use of the secure authorisation is conditional on agreement between the Director of Social Work and the Head of the named establishment. Young people are also admitted to secure care from courts either on remand for an alleged serious offence or by agreement with the Secretary of State, having been convicted of an indictable offence. On an annual basis about 40% of young people admitted to secure care come via the court system with the remainder being the responsibility of the Hearing system and social work departments.

The population of the small secure units would normally all be from the local area and their admission would be as a result of decisions by the Director of Social Work and the Head of the secure establishment clarified by a Hearing. As a result of the various routes into secure care, the normal population of a large secure unit is extremely mixed, which has major implications, not least for the education of the youngsters. The population at any one time is likely to consist of a mix of young people admitted from anything from one to seven days by Administrative Process; young people admitted on remand perhaps within hours of committing an alleged serious offence, who must be brought to trial within 110 days. Young people admitted from Children's Hearings on panel orders which must be reviewed within twenty-one days or three months. Young people convicted by courts, normally for indictable offences under Section 205 [for murder] or Section 206 of the Criminal Procedures [Scotland] Act 1975. Indictable offences include murder, culpable homicide, attempted murder, serious assault, rape, sexual assault, lewd and libidinous behaviour, arson and other serious crimes against property. In St Mary's at present sentences for indictable offences range from 1 year to 9 years under Section 206 and life under Section 205.

In my experience educational problems, although significant grounds at Children's Hearings for young people being considered for compulsory measures of care and education, rarely, if ever, are significant features in discussions concerning an admission to secure care. All children's residential establishments however have a statutory duty to ensure that children of school age in their care attend school. By the nature of a secure placement young people are obviously excluded from continuing their education in mainstream or special schooling and therefore secure units are obliged to provide education on the premises. In the smaller units teachers may visit to teach their pupils during their short period of detention or in some instances pupils can attend school under supervision within the establishment's education centre. Within large secure units education must be provided within the secure area.

If the function of secure provision was purely control and containment of troubled and troublesome young people, then the educational diet could be reduced to no more than keeping the young people occupied, quiet and in control. Child Care regulations set the general tasks of residential care as to meet 'young people's emotional, spiritual, intellectual and physical needs'. Residential care units are required to articulate a set of Aims and Objectives to demonstrate how these major tasks are achieved [Child Care Regulations 1983]. The Code of Practice insists that in large secure units 'a determined effort must be made to continue with formal education' and warns that 'unless suitable precautions are taken the children, many of whom will already have educational problems, will become even further disadvantaged during their stay in the secure unit'. Inspections by SWSG and the HMI of the large secure units have honed this advice down to a clear objective that such units should provide a balanced curriculum, which would aim to offer a range of educational experiences, common to all pupils of the same age and ability, as well as catering for the specific individual circumstances of each pupil.

In recent years developments in mainstream secondary education in Scotland have been based on modules of curriculum design comprising a number of modes of activity. These modes are outlined as linguistic and literacy study, mathematics, science, social studies, creative and aesthetic activities, physical activities, religious and moral studies and technological studies [SCCC guidelines]. There is now a clear expectation that educational provision is judged against these developments. Further, and rightly, there is an expectation that young people's educational opportunities should not be disadvantaged and that they therefore should have the normal opportunity to such certification in educational attainment either through SCE examinations or through National Certificates as offered by SCOTVEC modular courses. There is equally an expectation of and desire of staff within secure provision that recent developments for all pupils with special educational needs in special education and mainstream should be reflected in our practice. The full implications of the Five to Fourteen Report will, in due course, also be expected to illuminate educational thinking and strategies in the large secure units. As the officer in charge of such a unit I further expect all staff, including teaching staff, to be particularly aware and sensitive to issues concerning institutionalisation, dependency and addiction, sexuality, self-damaging behaviour, sexual abuse and a host of other areas of difficulty encountered by young people in our care.

Having outlined my expectations, those of external inspectors, referring agents and staff of secure units, we must now examine the reality of service provision and the obstacles to be overcome in achieving an adequate educational service for the young people.

The first major obstacles to the development of a suitably broad-based curriculum are the physical size of these institutions and the number of teaching staff who can, economically, be deployed to teach. No secure unit in Scotland enjoys the classroom space to reflect adequately recent curriculum advances, within my own unit there is a chronic shortage of classroom space, which drastically reduces the flexibility of our timetables as a vehicle for implementing curriculum enhancement. The largest educational staff group employed in secure care consists of ten full-time staff or their part-time equivalents, but their adequate deployment is hampered by the unsuitable nature of the accommodation. The introduction of job-share opportunities has certainly been significant as a means of augmenting the curriculum.

A further major set of obstacles to further challenge educational developments can be found by taking a closer look at the client group, particularly their length of stay within security, and their previous educational experience.

In 1990/91 the age range of pupils being educated at St Mary's varied from twelve years of age to sixteen plus. The ability range was from non-readers, with almost non-existent skills in numeracy, to young people being presented for Higher English and Maths. Previous school experience varied from almost perfect attendance up until the day of committing a serious offence to almost total non-attendance from leaving primary school. Analysis of statistics concerning lengths of stay at St Mary's in recent years show that 37% of residents remain only 7 days or less, 72% of young people are released after stays of 3 months and only 11% of residents stay longer than 1 year.

Readers, I hope, are now beginning to feel the sense of despair and panic that often accompanies senior educational staff discussions concerning educational strategies and developments. On a more positive note staffing resources are such that class sizes can be kept small, below those even of special schools outlined in national circulars. Within my own institution, education is seen as a challenging, life-long process, the collective responsibility of all staff, not only in the classroom setting, but in every situation and opportunity which arises. All staff are equally committed to establishing a stable living and working environment for the young people conducive to learning. Analysis of our client group has also formed the basis of our strategies which can and do change as results of admission trends.

Within St Mary's we have established a reception area within the classroom setting to accommodate all admissions for up to six weeks. This reception group offers a single base, a safe haven for new admissions, with two teachers largely concerned with settling young people into school routine and assessment. As many as 40% of our annual admissions do not progress beyond this point, but we have found this system beneficial.

Formal assessment coupled to the pupils self-assessment, is designed to take pupils two distinct routes, which are not necessarily mutually exclusive. Pupils who are likely to remain between 6 weeks and 1 year will enter courses in the National Certificate based on modules and half modules in all subject areas. The knowledge that certification can be achieved within a relatively short period of time has proved to be a great pupil motivator. Nothing succeeds better than success. Modular courses have also proved to be particularly relevant to young

Chapter 12

people taking up employment training or who go on to day release in colleges. The vast majority of young pupils leaving St Mary's enter the employment market rather than return to school. With an increase in the number of young people serving longer sentences we have also developed courses at the Standard Grade and Higher level to be able to offer this group a suitable challenge. Development across the width of the curriculum to match pupils' preferences and interests are impossible with a limited number of staff, but we have found voluntary tutors, either college lecturers or students, a very useful method of augmenting the basic educational diet. This also has the added advantage, in a closed community, of introducing new faces.

An on-going concern within the classroom setting is the need to assist young people who have missed large chunks of the normal educational process, but who show clear potential. We have developed a team teaching strategy to cope with sustaining such pupils within normal timetable. In some circumstances team teaching is not considered sufficient and individual pupils are withdrawn to be dealt with on a one-to-one basis.

With unlimited staff resources and accommodation we could do much more than we presently achieve. While I am not certain that adequate resources will ever be forthcoming, I am certain that the task of teaching special pupils will always require special, gifted and committed teachers. On a Monday morning at 9.30 am as young people leave their four units to go to school, I am always reminded of Shakespeare's reference to 'the whining school boy with his satchel and shining morning face, creeping like a snail unwillingly to school' [As You Like It - Act II] and this no matter how hard we try, the pupils always see our efforts causing them more seat, and even pain.

Postscript

Sur

Dougie Mackenzie

The wind battered the windows of the classroom, making the frames rattle like a pneumatic drill, sending the curtains billowing through the air and scattering piles of books and jotters.

'Somebody shut the window' shouted Mr Clink.

Half of 3C rushed to the back of the class and disappeared behind the curtains. Robert's face popped round.

'They're shut' he said.

Mr Clink got up and went to the back of the room. He stood in the corner as the wind brushed his face and stared at the closed window.

'How's that sur?' said Sylvia. 'It's blawin a gale.'

'Bad design' said Mr Clink. 'They don't build schools like they used to.'

He put his hand through the gap between the window frame and the wall. 'See.'

'That's terrible' said Debbie.

'Ma faither wull sort it fer ye' said Cherie. 'He's a brickie.'

'It's not as simple as that' said Mr Clink.

'How no?' said Debbie. 'Jist get a man up tae sort it.'

'It has to go through lots of committees and get approved before anyone can fix it. It takes months.'

'That's daft' said Cherie. 'Ma faither wull dae it the night.'

The building shook as a gust of wind butted the gable wall.

'D'ye think it'll fa doon?' said James Hunter.

'Ah'm feard' said Debbie.

'Maybe they'll send us hame' said Cherie.

'That *wull* be right' said James.

'O.K. open your jotters' said Mr Clink briskly, 'and turn to page 67 in your books. We're going to read the chapter about old Mrs Grant. Debbie, you read first.'

Debbie cleared her throat and waited for silence.

'*The social worker looked at his diary of the days work*' she read. '*Today he had a visit to old Mrs Grant. He was glad that Mrs Grant's daughter would be there. The last time...*'

Cherie put up her hand.

'Yes?' said Mr Clink.

'We've got a social worker' she said.

'Have you' said Mr Clink.

Postscript

'Aye. Ma faither wis batterin ma ma an the polis sent the social worker roond.'
'Her faither's mental' explained Debbie.
'Aye' said Billy. 'He gave me 50p at the fit o the stair last night. He wis steamin.'
'Let's get back to the subject' said Mr Clink. 'Read on Debbie.'
The last time he had visited the old lady she had shouted at him. She would not take the help he had offered. She said she needed no help from do gooders.
'Auld folk are like that' interrupted James Hunter. 'Awfu independent like. Ma granny wouldnae take meals on wheels. She said she wouldnae take anythin fer nuthin. She's 85 an still lives hersel.'
'Yes, old people are often very independent' said Mr Clink. 'They think any benefit they get from the state is charity.'
'Whits benefit?' said Louse.
'Things like child benefit and old age pensions.'
'Ah went tae a benefit match once' said Peter.
'That's not the same thing' said Mr Clink. 'But I want you all to think about the benefits that Mrs Grant is entitled to. Let's look at the social worker's case notes on Mrs Grant. Peter you read the next section. The one headed 'Money.''
'Money' read Peter slowly. *'Doesn't have enough (only retirement pension). House cold. Often goes to bed early to save on heating. Dog gets meat every day but she has toast and tea for many meals.'*
Karen put her hand up.
'Yes Louise.'
'Ah'm Karen sur. She's Louise.'
'Sorry Karen.'
Karen and Louise were identical twins.
'Ma sister's cat had six kittens.'
'That's very nice but what's that to do with...'
'She drooned them in the lavvy pan.'
'That's terrible' said Cherie.
'She tried tae strangle her bairn as well' said Karen.
'She must have a social worker like us then' said Cherie.
'Naw they took it aff her.'
Mr Clink cleared his throat loudly.
'Peter' he said 'Read.'
The catch on one of the groaning windows snapped. It broke loose from the frame, flapping and then hovering, held firmly in the hard fist of the gale. A small tornado whipped round the room, sending books and maps spinning through the air and onto the floor.
'Ah'll get it' shouted James Hunter.

He leapt up and grabbed the window catch as a gust of wind blew it out again, jerking him off his feet. For a moment he hung suspended above the tracing tables.

'Look' screamed Mary. 'He's taen aff.'

Mr Clink climbed up and seized the handle, pulling the window down.

'Get the janitor' he said to Robert.

'Ye looked jist like that wee man ah saw at Blackpool' said Mary to James. 'He wis shot oot a cannon intae the water.'

'Aye but he had a crash helmet' said Cherie

'How d'you ken?' said Mary.

'Ah wis there wi you wisn't ah' said Cherie.

James stood redfaced and breathless, his hair spiked by the wind.

'Ye look jist like Oor Wullie' said Sean.

'Shut it' said James. 'At least ah've got one.'

'Sur' chorused the girls. 'James Hunters bein rude.'

The janitor came and tied down the window with wire but it didn't seem to make much difference. The children weighted the bottom of the curtains with books to stop them getting tangled in the heads of those at the back.

'Ye could've lost yer finger' said Karen to James. 'Like me.'

She held up her forefinger which was severed above the knuckle. Mr Clink stared at it in disgust.

'How did that happen?' he asked.

'Ah pit it in the spokes o ma brither's bike.'

'When it was spinning?'

'Aye'

'That was a stupid thing to do.'

'He telt me tae.'

'Didn't the hospital sew it back on?'

'She threw it in the fire.'

She nodded to her sister.

'What on earth for?'

'Nae wonder' said Louise. 'It wis disgustin.'

'Let's read on' said Mr Clink. 'Let's find out if the old lady gets enough to eat. Robert, what does the social workers case notes say about the old lady's food.'

The wind thundered and the windows rattled.

Suggested meals on wheels to give one good meal a day read Robert.

'Hoi sur' shouted John. 'Whit did the wog say when the missionary drove intae the camp?'

'No racist jokes' said Mr Clink. 'Let's just get on with the lesson.'

'What did he say?' asked Sylvia.

'Ah, meals on wheels.'

Postscript

The class laughed.
'That's a barry one' said Cherie.
'She could eat rabbit' said Robert.
'What?'
'The auld wumman could eat rabbit. Ah gave the auld wifie next door rabbit last week. Ma whippet ripped its heid aff.'
'Where did you get the rabbit?' asked Mr Clink, interested.
'Ower the fields at night. Lampin ken. Aw ye need is a torch an a guid dug. Ye shine a light an when the dug chases a rabbit or a hare it runs intae it. It aye stops in the light. Then ye hit it ower the heid or else yer dug gets it.'
'That's cruel' said Diane. 'Puir wee rabbits.'
'Dinnae talk guff' said Robert. 'They're pests.'
'Pay attention' said Mr Clink. 'Let's concentrate on Mrs Grant. We've read all about her and she's got a lot of problems. Can anyone tell me what her problems are?'
'She's auld' said Michael.
'Aye, like you sur' said Jane.
'We're not talking about me and anyway I'm not old.'
'Ancient mair like' said Robert.
'D'you get a free bus pass sur?' said Michael.
'Look' said Mr Clink. 'Cut out the cheek and answer the question. What problems does an old person have?'
'Her mans deid' said Jane.
'Good. She's a widow and lives alone. We'll make a list. Put a heading in your jotter and underneath it we'll write our problems.'
He wrote OLD MRS GRANT on the blackboard.
'That's a miracle' said John.
'What is?' said Mr Clink.
'Ye've got a piece of chalk. It usually takes ye ten minutes tae find one.'
'Have ye got a pencil sur?' said James.
'Me as well' said Mary.
'Sur' said Michael. 'Ah need a pencil.'
'You're supposed to bring pencils' said Mr Clink.
'Ah did' said Jane. 'But somebody chored it.'
'Ah left mine in Maths' said Michael.
Mr Clink issued pencils.
'Let's write the first problem' he said. 'Lives alone. What else?'
'She's deid' said Robert.
'O.K.' said Mr Clink. 'Let's cut the comedy. Look at what's written on page 68.'

Silence.

'You're very quiet all of a sudden. Plenty to say until you're asked a question. Well, look at the sentence in the first paragraph. The social worker has written *Often goes to bed early*. Why?'

'Cos she's tired' said Debbie.

'Cos she's got a fancy man' said Robert.

'Any more wisecracks from you Robert and you're working on your own out in the corridor.'

'That could be right sur' said Sylvia. 'When ma grandfaither died ma granny got hersel a boyfriend. Ma faither went doon tae see her one mornin an the two of them were haen breakfast in bed.'

'Dirty pair o auld buggers' said Cherie.

'Watch your language Cherie' said Mr Clink.

'Sorry sur but nae wonder. Imagine carryin on at that age.'

'Look' said Mr Clink. 'I want a reason why she might go to bed early.'

'Tae sleep' said Cherie.

'In winter?' said Mr Clink.

'So she disnae sleep in' said Sylvia.

'But she's retired' said Debbie. 'She disnae have tae go tae work.'

'Ah ken' said James. 'Tae keep warm.'

'At last' said Mr Clink. 'Lots of old people nowadays find it hard to keep warm in winter. Why do they dread the winter?'

'What the winter?' said Debbie.

'Hate it' said Mr Clink.

'So dae ah' said Debbie. 'Our hoose is freezin.'

'Sur' said Mary. 'Ye want tae see the condensation in oor hoose. Ye cannae sleep in ma bedroom in winter.'

'We've got mushrooms on oor wa' said James.

'There you are' said Mr Clink. 'If you find it hard to keep warm in winter just think how hard it is for an old person.'

'Ah dinnae see how it can be any harder fer an auld person than it is fer us' said Cherie. 'If yer cauld yer cauld.'

'Old people are very susceptible to the cold' said Mr Clink.

'We're very respectable an a' said Jane.

'Does anyone know the kind of illness that old people are likely to get if they become too cold' said Mr Clink.

'Aids' said Robert.

'That's terrible that Aids' said Debbie. 'It's a ower the place.'

'It's the dirty needles that the junkies use' said Mary. 'Ye want tae see them at the foot o oor stair. Ma ma's feard tae go oot at night.'

Postscript

'Send yer faither doon tae them' said Robert.
'She disnae hae a faither' said Diane.
'Ah do so hae a faither' said Mary. 'An even if a dinnae at least he's no an auld alky like yours.'
'Silence' shouted Mr Clink. 'It's not Aids.'
'Ma ma an da were oot on Saturday night' said Sylvia. 'Oor babysitter an his girlfriend were in the lavvy shootin up heroin a night. He asked me if ah wanted some. When ah telt ma faither he wis right annoyed. 'Right' he said. 'That's the last time ah'll ask him tae babysit."
'It's everywhere that Aids' said Jane. 'Ah read in the Sunday Mail that we'll aw hae it in ten years. It's aw they poofs that's spreadin it.'
'Forget Aids' bawled Mr Clink.
The class was silent.
'What do people get if they become too cold?'
'Flu' said Michael.
'It's written in your books; on page 68" said Mr Clink.
'Arthritis' said James.
'The word I'm lookin for is hypothermia.'
He wrote it on the board.
'Never heard o it' said James.
'Is that no whit the junkies use?' said Mary.
'It's what happens to the body when it loses too much heat' said Mr Clink. 'What makes it serious is that you can suffer from it gradually over months without realising you've got it.'
'Cancer's like that sur' said Sylvia. 'Ma ma had cancer but she felt fine. Jist this lump inside her.'
'I'm sorry to hear that Sylvia' said Mr Clink.
'Oh she's awright noo sur' said Sylvia. 'She's been oot the hospital fer months. But she has tae dae the lavvy intae a bag.'
'Oh. Well I'm glad she's better.'
'Aye she's awright' said Sylvia. 'Only she's got tae go back fer an operation next week.'
'Oh.'
'She used tae be right fit. Noo she's as skinny as a rake.'
The bell rang.
'That's the bell sur' they all shouted.
'Put your seats in' said Mr Clink.
There was a scraping of seats and desks. Some hung round the door waiting to be dismissed. Others gathered round Mr Clink's desk for a last few moments of conversation.

'Ken the trouble wi this class sur?' said Robert.

'What?' said Mr Clink, trying to make a pile of books and jotters as they thudded onto his desk.

'We talk too much.'

'Yes' said Mr Clink. 'Class dismissed.'

Contributors

Joe Brown is a member of Strathclyde Region Psychological Service.

David Dean, OBE, is Principal of Raddery, a therapeutic community in the Highlands near Inverness.

Bill Duffy is Principal of St Mary's, Kenmure, an independent, secure residential centre for young people in care.

Deirdre Leach is Headteacher at Forteviot School in the Department of Child and Family Psychiatry, Royal Hospital for Sick Children, Edinburgh.

Gwynedd Lloyd is a lecturer at Moray House.

Andrew McCracken is Headteacher at Wellington, a residential school in Lothian Region.

Dougie McKenzie is a teacher seconded to Moray House from Lothian Region.

Alan McLean is a member of Strathclyde Region Psychological Service.

Hamish MacPhee is a member of Fife Region Psychological Service.

Sandy Peterson is a teacher seconded to Moray House from Lothian Region.

Tim Pickles is a freelance consultant with Framework, Scotland.

Malcolm Schaffer is Depute Regional Reporter to the Children's Panel in Lothian Region.

Dave Simpson is Coordinator of Panmure House, Lothian Region.

Barry Wilford is Project Leader of the Citadel Youth Project in Edinburgh.

'Ken the trouble wi this class sur?' said Robert.

'What?' said Mr Clink, trying to make a pile of books and jotters as they thudded onto his desk.

'We talk too much.'

'Yes' said Mr Clink. 'Class dismissed.'

Contributors

Joe Brown is a member of Strathclyde Region Psychological Service.

David Dean, OBE, is Principal of Raddery, a therapeutic community in the Highlands near Inverness.

Bill Duffy is Principal of St Mary's, Kenmure, an independent, secure residential centre for young people in care.

Deirdre Leach is Headteacher at Forteviot School in the Department of Child and Family Psychiatry, Royal Hospital for Sick Children, Edinburgh.

Gwynedd Lloyd is a lecturer at Moray House.

Andrew McCracken is Headteacher at Wellington, a residential school in Lothian Region.

Dougie McKenzie is a teacher seconded to Moray House from Lothian Region.

Alan McLean is a member of Strathclyde Region Psychological Service.

Hamish MacPhee is a member of Fife Region Psychological Service.

Sandy Peterson is a teacher seconded to Moray House from Lothian Region.

Tim Pickles is a freelance consultant with Framework, Scotland.

Malcolm Schaffer is Depute Regional Reporter to the Children's Panel in Lothian Region.

Dave Simpson is Coordinator of Panmure House, Lothian Region.

Barry Wilford is Project Leader of the Citadel Youth Project in Edinburgh.

Chapter 11

Education in a Psychiatric Setting

Deirdre Leach

For a minority of children a short spell of residential treatment in a psychiatric unit enables assessment and treatment to be given with the necessary intensity and immediacy.

In Lothian the in-patient unit of the Department of Child and Family Psychiatry is Forteviot. The average length of admissions is four months. Weekends spent at home and daily contact with family through visits, family therapy sessions and phone calls ensure that the child's place is kept for him and that problems continue to be seen within the context of the family even after admission. Referrals are made initially to the out-patient department mainly by general practitioners and the Royal Hospital for Sick Children but they also come from the Departments of Social Work and Education Psychology. On average 800 new referrals are seen at DCFP in a year. Of these only an average of 35 children are admitted to Forteviot.

The decision to remove a child from his home and his school for a period of in-patient assessment and treatment is not one that is ever taken lightly.

Reasons for admission
Often the reason for admission is likely to be that home - or clinic - based treatment has not proved sufficient. It is sometimes impossible to make an accurate assessment when a family is seen at fortnightly intervals for one hour sessions. Or it may be that no change has been effected by the various interventions and the reason for this failure has not become clear. Intensive observation of the child in the different settings within the in-patient unit is therefore necessary.

Sometimes it is obvious that a child will not have his needs met effectively nor will his family be able to survive *except* through a brief and positive experience of separation and treatment of the child in a residential setting (Wells 1991). This gives both child and family a badly needed period of respite and time to offer family therapy in the hope of restoring the family intact. It takes the pressure off the child and gives him a chance to recover some of his self-esteem which will have been eroded by feelings of blame, shame, failure and guilt.

Examples of referrals from RHSC may be eating disorders, encopresis or chronic pain which will have been investigated for physical cause but found to have associated emotional aspects. Or there may be a physical or neurological problem such as diabetes or epilepsy which in itself would not require psychiatric intervention but may be interrelated with emotional and behavioural disturbance. Children who suffer from such illnesses are obviously more vulnerable although of course many cope well particularly if they have good support at home and in school.

Fortunately children suffering from a truly psychotic illness are rare. In the last ten years there have only been seven children showing schizophrenic behaviour.

Educational problems alone would not constitute a reason for in-patient admission but again where they are related to emotional and behavioural difficulties which is a common feature a child may be admitted in order for a clear assessment to be made and the appropriate help given in all areas, not only in school.

Barker (1974) sees the reason for admission to an in-patient unit as follows:

(1) Altering the family dynamics by the temporary removal of one member.
(2) Demonstrating to the family that the child does have the capacity to change in a way which they have come to believe is impossible.
(3) Relieving temporarily the family, school or community of a child with whom they are unable to cope, and
(4) Enabling normal emotional growth and maturation to proceed where formerly adverse environmental factors were preventing this.

By (1) above, altering family dynamics, it is possible to get a clearer picture of what part the disturbed/disturbing behaviour plays. For example one fairly common phenomenon is when a child has become a "scapegoat" in a family. This is an unconscious process and might occur when there are perhaps marital difficulties. Rather than acknowledge the actual existing problems in the relationship it might be that each parent focuses negative feelings such as anger, frustration, disappointment or resentment onto a particular child. It becomes a chicken-and-egg situation because the child will have long ago begun to respond to these attitudes and indeed may have in some way attracted them by behaving badly. When the child is admitted to the unit several things can happen:

- the parents are forced to look at their marital problems
- a sibling may become the scapegoat thus proving the hypothesis
- the child is given a positive, supportive and rewarding experience which helps him change his view of himself and consequently his behaviour.

Barker's third point now seems rather a negative reason for admission and hopefully in the 1990s it is more likely that support systems will be built in to enable family, school and community to work with a very difficult child. Unfortunately there are not always the resources for this to happen in a way which will really benefit the child. Then it is better for the child for him to be removed from an increasingly negative and perhaps hostile environment - a time for everyone to draw breath.

The word 'normal' in (4) above seems like an anomaly as a psychiatric unit is not a normal environment! However, as with a plant in a hothouse, a child can be taken through normal developmental stages emotionally, socially and educationally at an intensive and accelerated rate. Provided certain changes are effected in the child's own environment he can then continue to make progress on discharge from the unit.

The Unit

Forteviot is staffed by a consultant psychiatrist, nurses, occupational therapists and teachers, with therapeutic input from outpatient staff including social workers and clinical psychologists. There are eighteen places for children ranging from late infancy to early adolescence.

An eclectic approach is adopted in the unit drawing on behavioural, cognitive and psychodynamic techniques. Family therapy accounts for a high proportion of staff input. Multidisciplinary skills are utilized in treatment programmes.

Residential treatment can provide a very powerful tool in that the therapeutic potential of groups can be made use of.

In Forteviot the multidisciplinary management team meet weekly to discuss referrals and to decide on placing and timing of admissions.

All children referred must have a home base and all problems are seen in the context of the family, school and community.

Recent developments in the Health Board in terms of audit and contracting have necessitated in the department being more definitive about the categories of disorder treated in Forteviot. In many ways this will be useful to outside agencies in that it will be possible to state clearly what it is the unit has to offer.

The categories include various types of conduct disorders, encopresis, eating disorders, school refusal, severe emotional disorders such as depressive states with suicidal ideas, sleep disorders, pre-pubertal psychosis and somatisation disorders such as hysterical paralysis.

Children with continuing and significant aggressive disorders, which are in effect control issues, are not felt to be appropriately placed in a psychiatric unit.

Definition

Wolff (1971) states that there is no universally applicable definition of emotional disturbance in children. It is many ways depends on the perception of the problem and the level of tolerance. Behaviour which would not be seen as out of place in one school setting might seem quite outrageous in another. Serious difficulties arise when stresses are overwhelming for a child and then his reactions can be viewed as "normal" in that any child would react similarly under these conditions.

The definition of psychiatric disorder given by Rutter is as follows: "marked and prolonged abnormalities of behaviour, emotions or relationships sufficient to give rise to handicap which might affect the family, community or child". (Rutter 1967)

It is important to remember that a psychiatric diagnosis describes the problem a child has and is not a description of the child.

The School

The school is seen as an integral part of the treatment package.

In Forteviot there are three classes, two primary and one secondary, of no more than six children in each. Although on Health Board premises the school itself is run by Lothian Region Special Education Department.

Children have a normal school week. In most other psychiatric units in Scotland part-time schooling is provided. Often this is due to having separate groups of day-patients and in-patients. By providing full-time education not only are the children given the maximum opportunity to receive help with school work but also it means that reintegration into mainstream should be easier.

Teachers contribute to the overall assessment and provide important information on classroom behaviour and peer relationships but obviously their particular expertise is in the educational assessment. This encompasses areas such as work attack, concentration, self-esteem, independence, maturational level, motor control, creativity and problem-solving. It looks at how the child responds to new situations, to praise or reproach, to explanations and new information, to different teaching strategies and so on.

The teacher elicits information about how best to ensure enough success and enjoyment with which to motivate the child without putting too much pressure on him. (Leach 1990)

As with any school for children with emotional and behavioural difficulties there is a dilemma about curricular balance. Children attending a school in a psychiatric unit come from a wide variety of backgrounds. In one class there might be a child from a special school working alongside a child from a high-flying fee-paying school. It is important therefore to gear each child's educational experience to his own needs.

It might be that one child is not ready to settle in class, is completely unmotivated and cannot concentrate on a given task. This being the case work must be aimed at these aspects before the teacher can expect any progress academically.

Another child's problem may be that of overstretching himself, seeing everything as competition perhaps as the result of parental pressure. As part of the overall treatment he would be helped to take part in activities for the sake of enjoyment.

Emphasis is put on the value of education in the unit and it is viewed as a primary treatment modality. In a wide sense education itself can be seen as therapy in that self-esteem is raised through increased success in academic and practical skills, improved communication and problem-solving abilities. (Leach 1990)

The curriculum followed in the two primary classes is the same as in mainstream schools. There are visiting art and music teachers. A full computer system in each classroom ensures that all children become familiar with its use.

The aim in the secondary class is to provide as wide a curriculum as would be found in a top primary class with emphasis on language and maths. Many of the children of secondary age require remedial help.

Teachers aim to provide continuity of curriculum where possible. The Forteviot teacher liaises with the child's guidance teacher and where there are no educational problems time in school is spent profitably on work provided by the child's own school. Independent study skills, discussion techniques, creative writing, expressive arts, problem solving, knowledge of current affairs and social skills are all areas for development in the small group.

Educational provision in residential psychiatric units seems to vary considerably in style and delivery. R W McKay (1987) visited units in Scotland and found that regional authorities varied widely in their management response to this provision. He found that in units where the curriculum was neither documented nor completely appropriate poor credibility was accorded to teaching staff who played a relatively lower profile in terms of their contribution to treatment and planning.

Fortunately the converse is true. In Forteviot priority is given to the school day when therapy sessions are planned and disruption of classes is kept to a minimum.

Communication
In order for an admission to work well there has to be good communication both within the department and outwith. It is crucial that there are clearly defined channels of communication.

The pre-admission procedure is important. So that as much information as possible is obtained a home visit and sometimes a school visit is arranged.

A pre-admission case discussion to which outside agencies such as Educational Psychology, Social work, and Community Health, are invited is set up. A treatment plan is worked out then and everyone is made aware of his remit and of the aims of admission. It is not possible at this stage to decide on length of admission. Generally an assessment takes about six weeks and treatment is based on that assessment.

The child visits the unit about one week prior to admission. Parents are of course free to turn down the offer of admission but this rarely happens.

Mid-week visits by parents and weekends home are seen as an important part of the assessment and treatment. Parents are expected to share with nursing staff any concerns they may have or progress they have noticed in the child's behaviour or in the family functioning. At the weekend both child and family practise new behaviour or new skills leaned during the week and results are reported back. Such tasks may take the form of limit-setting by parents, or of the child mixing socially with peers in the community.

Nursing staff work with parents of the younger children on management issues by using modelling techniques. They model limit-setting, how to play with the child, how to communicate clearly and simply how to relax and enjoy interacting with the child. The sessions can take the form of a structured activity in the ward or outings to supermarkets, cafes, on public transport etc. One nurse is assigned to work with, most commonly, the mother as principal caretaker.

Teachers from the child's own school are welcome to visit the child during the school day. It is important that the Forteviot teacher and the child's own teacher have opportunities to discuss progress, assessment and methods used in any remediation process.

Within the unit there are various meetings ensuring that all inpatient staff are aware of, for example, reports of weekends home or progress being made in therapy sessions.

Case discussions are held at intervals on each child. Reports are heard from the nurse, teacher, occupational therapist, individual therapist and family therapist. Any test results are reported and the overall assessment fits together like a jigsaw.

On discharge an objective educational report is sent to the child's school. Follow-up sessions are arranged in the clinic or in the child's community. Again it is crucial that adequate information is passed on to the appropriate workers. There can be difficulties with respect to confidentiality due to the medical nature of the work. However most parents see the need for handover of information.

Children's Communication

Much of the work of a psychiatric unit is aimed at helping the child communicate feelings and thoughts as well as helping the child to change his behaviour. A variety of therapies are used in Forteviot: individual, play, behaviour, family, cognitive and group.

Useful techniques and principles can be adopted from several of these and modified for use in the classroom. Behavioural methods have become well established in schools and provide a useful framework in terms of clear thinking towards defining the problem, rewarding appropriate behaviour, etc.

Play therapy, cognitive therapy and group work in the form of social skills training have much to offer teachers of emotionally and behaviourally disturbed children provided appropriate training is given. The techniques should be used to enhance teaching methods and to help the child to help himself. They should not be used in an attempt to expose a child's inner self. The classroom is no place for any form of intensive individual therapy which might leave the child feeling fragile and vulnerable to his peers.

Children benefit from opportunities to express themselves through music, art and drama as well as through creative writing in school. Children have few words for emotions and therefore are limited in their ability to conceptualize situations. By developing their vocabulary and providing experience through role-play and social skills games, children are helped to think in terms of a continuum of feelings and to understand variability in mood not only in themselves but hopefully in others. (Leach 1990)

Training

In order to maintain a therapeutic milieu a well-integrated consistently applied programme is needed.

To this end many opportunities are made available to all staff to attend workshops and lectures and an in-service training programme covers theory and practice of, for example, the various forms of therapy. *Ad hoc* lectures are set up at short notice to deal with any topic causing concern in the unit such as anorexia nervosa, sexual abuse, epilepsy.

In a multidisciplinary setting roles overlap considerably although each discipline contributes its own particular skills and retains its own identity. Shared training addresses the need for a consistent approach throughout the unit and helps to combat splitting and manipulation of staff by children. It also serves to keep staff interested and informed which in turn motivates. Due to the training needs of psychiatric staff the whole unit benefits from up-to-date information on research and new ideas.

The way forward

In the seventies emphasis began to shift away from the search for problems, pathology and negative factors in the patient and family and to move towards identifying assets and positive attributes with which to work (Wardle 1991).

The 1990s are bringing more community-based work, promoting resilience in the child and protective factors in school and in society. More preventive work in schools and children's centres in the form of social skills groups or parents' management training groups would be beneficial as would an increase in teachers' in-service training focussing on issues of emotional, behavioural and psychological disturbance.

The Nuffield Child Psychology and Psychiatry Unit in collaboration with the Department of Education of the University of Newcastle-Upon-Tyne run a joint course for nurses and teachers. Interdisciplinary training using established programmes in psychiatric units is not only an efficient deployment of resources but advantageous in that the focus is wider than it would be for a specific profession.

Social work and education services are now working more closely together in most areas of Scotland. It is to be hoped that this decade will signal the coming together of clinicians and educationalists. If the concept of the 'whole' child in the context of his home, school and community is to be meaningful this would seem to be the best way forward.

Concerted effort is needed by all disciplines and agencies to understand each other's differences and work together. Differences of approach and practice can be viewed positively and can lead to healthy evolution as long as opinions are not held with delusional fervour.

Wardle (1991) tabulates some of the more exaggerated splits in child psychiatry. He entitles the table 'Maleficent Dichotomies' because of the harm they have done in depriving children of balanced care and child rearing. Wardle suggests that if 'versus' is removed from the table we are left with a list of concepts and strategies comprising a comprehensive service for children. None need be in opposition or worse still, competition!

Methods/Ideas		*Counter-Methods/Counter Ideas*
Nature	v.	Nurture
Behaviourism	v.	Psychoanalysis
Psychological methods	v.	Medical methods
Child guidance	v.	Hospital child psychiatry
Residential treatment	v.	Community treatment

Family therapy	v.	Individual therapy
Control & discipline	v.	Loving nurture
Professional autonomy	v.	Team work
Confidentiality	v.	Open communication
Audit & good management	v.	Professional freedoms
Measurement & scientific methods	v.	Descriptive humanitarian methods
Belief in standards	v.	Tolerance of deviance
Educational methods	v.	Therapeutic method

McKay (1987) identifies a lack of evidence to suggest that the teaching within psychiatric wards or residential schools does provide special or effective teaching. Howlin (1985) states: 'Vague and untested notions of providing social therapy abound and education is often neglected'.

There is obviously a need for research into the area of educational provision in psychiatric units throughout Britain not only to allay such generalised misconceptions but also to identify and build on existing good practice.

References

Barker, P (1974). *The Residential Psychiatric Treatment of Children*. Crosby Lockwood Staple. London.

Barker, P (1986). *Basic Child Psychiatry, 4th Edition*. Collins.

Howlin, P (1985). Special educational treatment. In Rutter, M and Hersov, L (eds) *Child and Adolescent Psychiatry: Modern Approaches, 2nd Edition*. Blackwell. London.

Leach, D (1990). Teaching in a psychiatric unit. In Bovair, K and Baker, D (eds) *Making the the Special Schools Ordinary? Volume 2*. The Falmer Press.

McKay, R (1987). Educational provision in residential psychiatric units. SED final report: *Educational Psychologists' Professional Development Initiative*.

Rutter, M, Tizard, J and Whitmore, K (1970). *Education, Health and Behaviour*. Longman.

Wardle, C J (1991). Twentieth century influences on the development in Britain of services for child and adolescent psychiatry. *British Journal of Psychiatry 159*. Pp 53-68.

Wells, P (1992). Survival in a cold climate. *Psychiatric Bulletin 16*. Pp 10-14.

Wolff, S (1971). *Children Under Stress*. Penguin.